Dear Highlights

Dear Highlights

What Adults Can Learn from 75 Years of Letters and Conversations with Kids

Christine French Cully

FOREWORD BY AMY DICKINSON

Highlights Press
Honesdale, Pennsylvania

Copyright © 2021 by Highlights for Children
All rights reserved. Copying or digitizing this book for storage, display, or distribution in any other medium is strictly prohibited.

For information about permission to reprint selections
from this book, please contact permissions@highlights.com.

Published by Highlights Press
815 Church Street
Honesdale, Pennsylvania 18431
ISBN: 978-1-64472-325-8
eBook ISBN: 978-1-64472-390-6
Library of Congress Control Number: 2021932932
Manufactured in: Crawfordsville, IN, USA
Manufacturing date: 06/2021

First edition
Visit our website at Highlights.com.
10 9 8 7 6 5 4 3 2 1

Design and Art Direction: Red Herring Design
Production: Margaret Mosomillo, Jessica Berger, and Lauren Garofano
Cover Design: Red Herring Design
Cover Illustration: Serge Bloch
Interior Illustrations: Serge Bloch, Nic Farrell, Travis Foster, and Julie Wilson

Photo credits: 89studio (66); Super Cat (143); koosen (211, 276); Pakhnyushchy (46, 51, 159, 193, 212, 250, 257); Picsfive (27, 32, 38, 50, 60, 70, 96, 111, 126, 135, 145, 150, 152, 170, 198, 200, 204, 214, 216, 219, 236, 240, 244, 260, 266, 270, 298); photastic (69, 84, 121, 141, 168, 194, 232, 275); Marko Poplasen (100, 156, 268, 276); showcake (44, 58, 72, 114, 130, 160, 172, 196, 214, 230, 262, 272, 286, 300, 308); spacezerocom (40, 102, 134, 158, 177, 208, 228, 237); Suradech Prapairat (29, 62, 74, 112, 117, 120, 122, 130, 132, 147, 168, 170, 185, 230, 259, 274, 284); Tartila (84, 141, 258, 262, 275); Taty Vovchek (128)

To my wonderful children, Matt and Ali. Being your mother has been the great joy of my life.

And to all the children who have written to *Highlights* to share their hopes and dreams, their worries and fears, and their joys and sorrows, big and small. Thank you for sharing your voices with us. We are honored.

CONTENTS

Foreword

ADVICE COLUMNISTS OCCUPY A STRANGE AND RARIFIED space in the world of words; unlike therapists or physicians, we operate more or less as trusted best friends or honorary aunties and uncles to the people who write to us for advice. Our most important gift is to gain, and retain, insight—and to pass it along. We are amateurs, armed mainly with a way with words, a knack for paying close attention, and the ability to disseminate wisdom, along with our capacity to care about people we don't know personally—and will never meet. In fact, the only thing we really know about the people who write to us is that they have the courage to ask, along with a desire to be heard and understood.

Once upon a time, we were all children. Understanding, compassion, and respect are paramount—especially when responding to questions from children. No column has ever done this better than "Dear Highlights," the long-running column in beloved *Highlights* magazine.

The spectrum of questions tackled by the magazine since its founding in 1946 spans what I see as the North and South Poles of human experience: Love and Loss. And because these questions are being asked by brave and curious children, the questions themselves are simple, beautiful, honest, and without the artifice, manipulative sheen, or flat-out ego that I so often see in queries sent to my own "Ask Amy" advice column, which is geared toward adults. (The gift of authenticity that comes along with childhood is too often lost with the passage of time.)

To read questions sent by children over the decades expressing concern over so many terrifying events—from assassinations of national leaders, to terrorist bombings, natural disasters, police brutality, and to the coronavirus pandemic—is a reminder of how traumatic and overwhelming these events can be for children, and how important it is that adults respond honestly and with great care.

To read questions about the quotidian concerns of childhood— how to manage siblings, schoolyard bullies, parents, friendships, or how to convince their folks to get them a pet—is to absorb the beautiful universality of our more common experiences.

We have so much to learn from these kids. The thoughtful editors of "Dear Highlights" know this, because the answers to these thousands of queries always illuminate the legitimacy of the question, as well as provide such supportive, compassionate, and timeless advice!

To read questions about the quotidian concerns of childhood . . . is to absorb the beautiful universality of our more common experiences.

What I didn't know before reading this book was that the editors of *Highlights* magazine respond to every single query sent to them—not just those that are published. I can guarantee that the tens of thousands of children who have received a personal reply over the decades have treasured this very special correspondence. This legacy of caring cannot be measured; it can only be felt.

As the mother and stepmother to five daughters, every single page of this treasured collection moves me profoundly. But what brings me to tears, again and again, are the facsimiles of the letters themselves, the handwritten poems on notebook paper, and the lovely illustrations sent in by children—who painstakingly express their hopes, dreams, fears, stresses, and triumphs to the wise and wonderful team behind "Dear Highlights." What a joy to see this authentic and creative work shared on the page!

To read these questions and answers—some from many years ago— makes one yearn to know how things turned out for the children who so bravely told their stories and asked their questions to the magazine. Read this opening sentence from the year 2000, written by a twelve-year-old girl named Lara, whose relationship with her mother was brutal: "I am writing on behalf of my feelings, which are buried so deep inside of me . . ." Did the compassionate response to Lara's plea make her feel heard and realize that she is

What we do know for sure is that the wisdom embedded in these thousands of "Dear Highlights" Qs & As has radiated outward and helped unknown scores of children and caregivers who have had the good fortune to read *Highlights*.

deserving of love? (And—I can't help wondering: Did Jake—age 9—ever stop cussing?)

What we do know for sure is that the wisdom embedded in these thousands of "Dear Highlights" Qs & As has radiated outward and helped unknown scores of children and caregivers who have had the good fortune to read *Highlights*. For every person who asks a question, there are all those who have the same question or concern but don't share it.

In times of great stress or trouble, Mr. Rogers advised children: "Look for the helpers. You will always find people who are helping." That's exactly what children writing to "Dear Highlights" find when they put pen to paper: Helpers whose open-minded trust and kindness surely has made our world a better place.

February 2021
Amy Dickinson
Freeville, NY

Where the
Conversation Began

HEN A CHILD SHARES THEIR INNER THOUGHTS, we are given a gift. It's an honor and a responsibility —even a sacred trust. Through letters, emails, poems, and drawings, hundreds of thousands of kids have engaged with *Highlights* magazine since its inception. They have shared their thoughts and feelings with us as if we were close friends. They write about the various challenges of growing up—difficulties at school, at home, and with peers. They write about their hopes and dreams. They write about their worries and fears—for themselves, for the people they love, and for the larger world. They ask, "What should I do?" "Can you help?" "What do you think?"

Since our beginning, it has been a Highlights tradition to read every letter and respond to every child. This practice has created for us an ongoing, authentic dialogue with children. It became a way to keep our finger on the pulse of kids—to stay attuned to their thoughts and feelings. It has led to our becoming a touchstone for generations of children navigating the ups and downs of childhood.

Our dedication to answering every child's letter is rooted in the views of the first editor and cofounder of *Highlights* magazine, Dr. Garry Cleveland Myers. A child psychologist, lifelong educator, and particularly astute observer of children, Dr. Myers believed that positive human relationships were a powerful motivator for children. He and Caroline Clark Myers, his educator wife and cofounder, were advocates for conversations with children that allowed adults to hear and understand kids' perspectives. In his many writings for adults, Dr. Myers urged parents to take pleasure in their children by being "appreciative listeners" and encouraging their kids to share their thoughts more often.

This philosophy of child-rearing was foundational to the magazine. It was apparent in the very first issue in 1946. By writing (for 25 years!) a monthly editor's message that welcomed kids to each new issue, Dr. Myers set the long Highlights tradition of speaking directly and conversationally with children. In his "Talks with the Editor" feature, which was later renamed "Let's Talk Things Over," he laid a foundation of trust and encouraged kids to self-reflect. This space in the magazine reinforced the idea that talking and communicating with people you trust are good ways to handle problems.

In those early years, our mailbag mostly held fan mail from kids, their queries about *Highlights*, and letters to Sammy Spivens—a puppet character in a long-running feature who encouraged kids to reflect on their bad habits.

But over time, we began to receive more and more letters from kids that revealed their thoughts and feelings. They wrote about difficulties in getting along with their friends and siblings, their career aspirations, being teased, caring for pets, societal concerns, and other topics that had a direct effect on them. From time to time, a page of their letters made it into an issue, and we began to see that kids were very interested in reading letters from other children. In 1979, we began publishing them in a regular advice column that continues today as "Dear Highlights."

It has led to our becoming a touchstone for generations of children navigating the ups and downs of childhood.

Throughout the evolution of the magazine over the years, as mail flowed in from kids—thousands of letters, drawings, and poems monthly—members of the editorial staff were specially trained in how to respond to them. No one took lightly the task of answering a child's letter. Rather, it was considered an honor and a basic tenet of the company's core beliefs: When a child writes to you, you write back with care and respect.

Eventually, we realized that we possessed a treasure trove of

information about childhood derived from a primary source—kids themselves. We saw research value in our reader mail, and we began to save it all. When the attic of our editorial offices, where the letters were stored, began to overflow, we contacted The Ohio State University. The staff in the Rare Books and Manuscripts Library saw the value in our collection of correspondence from children, which included letters, poems, drawings, stories, and science questions. Ohio State also recognized its historical significance, so they agreed to retain the letters in a special collection. Because they were unable to accept the total amount of mail we had amassed, we sent all the letters and emails we received from children, and one drawing and poem for every ten received— mostly from 1981 to the present. This archive was the main source for most of the kids' correspondence reproduced or excerpted here.

As we pored over the letters in the making of this book, we began to see a pattern that wasn't surprising: Kids' concerns have changed very little. Certainly, the world has changed dramatically since we received those first letters from kids, but how children grow has not. For 75 years, kids across generations have written to us about the same fundamental issues, still hoping for adult guidance and encouragement.

Given the consistency we saw in kids' letters over time, we were surprised to see more change in how we responded. We uncovered some replies that probably were too reflective of the different personalities of the editors who wrote them. Some letters may have called for more empathy than we offered in our briefer replies. We took too long to rephrase our suggestion to "talk this over with your parents" to "talk this over with a parent," to be sensitive to the growing number of readers living in single-parent households. We struggled— and still do—about our tendency to assume that the child who writes to us has at least one loving, caring parent or guardian. But we know that's not true for every child. Looking through a present-day lens, we sometimes wished we had answered a particular letter from another era a little differently. Yet, our belief that kids matter and what they think matters is at the very heart of every response. Sifting through the store of replies felt like looking at a series of snapshots taken over the decades, revealing both who *Highlights* was and is.

For some children, an in-person conversation with a trusted adult isn't possible, hasn't proved helpful, or seems too daunting to initiate.

What also remained consistent over time is the authenticity of a child's letter. They have come to us in childish scrawls, with misspellings and grammatical errors—or, more commonly in earlier years, in careful cursive. But, in 2006, for the first time, the number of emails eclipsed the number of postal letters we received—a trend that continued for about ten years.

Although many kids seem to find emails easier to write and send, we find that postal letters are easier to answer. When a child writes to us with paper and pencil, they sometimes give us additional contextual clues. We might be able to roughly guess the letter writers' age by looking at the handwriting, for example, which greatly helps us formulate a response. Often a child illustrates their letter, and the details in the drawing can offer hints about the problem not expressed in words. Some children forego a written message entirely and just send drawings about an upsetting event or situation. This was especially common after 9/11, when we received numerous drawings of airplanes hitting the Twin Towers. We responded to these drawings as if they were letters expressing worry or sadness.

Emails offer no such clues. Sometimes they don't even include the child's real name. The brevity and more anonymous feel to these notes make composing a meaningful response even more challenging.

Certainly, the ideal way to connect with kids is through face-to-face communication, which allows us to look them in the eyes and punctuate our response with supportive body language and warm hugs. But for some children, an in-person conversation with a trusted adult isn't possible, hasn't proved helpful, or seems too daunting to initiate. For them, writing a message to us serves.

Most children write to us only once, but some write to us several times. One reader, who found it particularly hard to navigate relationships with family and peers, wrote to us regularly over the course of ten years, beginning from age 7. In 2004, he sent us 33 postal letters—and, later, for a period, a daily email. All told, we sent him more than 200 replies. After a while, he

started to feel a little like family, and today the staff often wonders aloud how he is doing.

While the majority of our conversations with kids cover the common, daily challenges of childhood, some of the letters and emails are about serious or especially sensitive issues. In these cases, we seek the help of experienced, credentialed professionals, who are more than willing to review our replies. They help ensure that we're sending the best possible advice based on the information we have. As required by law, when kids tell us about abuse or neglect, we report it to the proper authorities. We handle emails in strict compliance with the Children's Online Privacy and Protection Act (COPPA). The names of the children whose letters are published in this book have been changed to protect their privacy. We've also preserved the integrity of each letter and reply we selected, leaving the original wording and spelling. We've cut text only to shorten when necessary.

This book is a powerful reminder that childhood is a period of heavy lifting for kids. . . . When we *hear* them, we learn how to better serve them.

In my long tenure at *Highlights*, I personally have read and responded to thousands of letters and emails from children. This remains a favorite part of my work as editor in chief. I am rarely surprised by any letter, but I am still frequently touched. Nevertheless, seeing so many messages from generations of kids bound together in a single volume moves me deeply. This book is a powerful reminder that childhood is a period of heavy lifting for kids. In their often brief but always intimate letters, we see how hard they work to develop their character, find belonging, discover their strengths, and build self-esteem.

If the archive at Ohio State is a time capsule, then this book is a tapestry. Pulling from some of the most beautiful threads of our correspondence over the decades, we have tried to weave together the letters, poems, and drawings shared with us into a depiction of childhood that's honest and rich in color and texture. Like the best art, it should stir you. Cause you to reflect. Make you feel the world of childhood.

I also hope this book spurs you to action—to commit to leaning in and listening to kids on their way to growing up. When we *hear* them, we learn how to better serve them. When we respond with thought and care, we model the way we hope they'll show up for others. By doing so, we ensure that childhood is the nurturing, positive experience kids need and deserve. This is how we put children on the path to becoming people who will help create a better world for all. We implore you to listen.

Letters About

Family

FAMILY, SCHOOL, AND FRIENDS ARE THE MAIN INFLUENCES on a child's life. Of these three, family is the single most important one. Children depend on family for all the necessities of life—food, shelter, love, trust, and security—beginning even before their first breath and continuing for at least a couple of decades. Kids' understanding of the most important qualities in relationships takes root at home with the family. Their early experiences at home, learning that they are safe and cared for and feeling like they belong, have an enduring effect on their well-being.

Family can be defined in several ways. Some define it simply as a group of people who share legal or genetic bonds, but at Highlights we define family as a group of people connected by the bonds of deep caring and commitment. It's the group of people with whom we share, usually, the same daily routines, rituals, and significant events. But at its center, family is the collection of people who nurture us and offer us love and support. It's the people who help us figure out who we are and where we fit in the world. This more inclusive definition encompasses the many different configurations of people whom our readers today call family.

In the early years of *Highlights*, the simple definition may have described most of our readers, who were part of nuclear families consisting of two opposite-gender parents still in their first marriage. In the 1960s, the apex of the post–World War II baby boom, this setting described 73 percent of all children in the U.S. But today, only 46 percent of kids live in this family structure.

These days, one in four mothers are raising kids on their own, and common family makeups include stepparent, grandparent, multiracial, LGBTQ parent, co-parent, and single-parent households. Divorce, which hit an all-time high in the 1970s and early 1980s (as did our reader mail about divorce), is still a factor, but the recent trend of fewer millennials choosing to marry is also an influence. In almost half of households headed by a married couple, both parents are working full-time. Often, the mother is the primary breadwinner. Family size is shrinking. In fact, the fastest growing American family structure is only-child families.

But despite all the change in how families are built, families continue to mean everything to kids. We're reminded of this when we ask young kids whom they most admire and they respond, typically, by naming a close family member. We also see their devotion in the drawings, poems, and letters about family life, which we've been receiving for years.

Kids' love for family, especially their parents, can be fierce, and their fear of losing a parent can be intense. Cheng, age 9 in 2014, wrote about his concern for his father's health. "My dad keeps smoking, and I want him to stop. It could easily kill him, and I want him to stop this bad habit." Perhaps even more common is the fear of losing a parent through divorce. One anonymous reader sent an email in 2008 to say that her parents were always fighting. "Do they still love me?" she wondered, "Because I have to pick one parent."

Many of the letters that kids write today about family life cover the same ground as previous generations of children wrote about. Kids still write to share some of the joys of family living, such as making room for a new baby or creating a fun vacation memory. They still write with objections to their bedtime, chores, allowance, and other family rules, although today they may expect to have more to say about how these decisions are made. And although much was made about the trend of helicopter parenting in the early 2000s and,

a few decades later, about drone parenting, we still receive letters from kids who crave more understanding and attention from their parents. In recent years, a primary parental distraction often seems to be an electronic device. In 2012, a reader named Joshua wrote, "My dad never wants to do anything fun with me anymore. After dinner, he just sits at his computer and reads the news."

Few children get through childhood without fighting with parents. The kids who write to us sometimes say that the arguments make them feel stressed or anxious, but usually they are writing for help in

Many of the letters that kids write today about family life cover the same ground as previous generations of children wrote about.

thinking about the conflict and seeking resolution. Some letters illustrate the tension between kids who want more freedom and parents who wish to keep them closely tethered to home.

Kids with siblings have, for decades, written to ask for help in coping with the unwanted attention of younger brothers and sisters. Living with siblings gives kids meaningful experience in developing patience and in accepting and tolerating differences in the habits and interests of others. But kids, of course, don't always see this as an upside to having bothersome siblings. Even if they do, it doesn't necessarily make getting along any easier. Kids who feel jealous of siblings whom they perceive to be getting more love and attention often write to have their feelings heard and acknowledged. Children who write about older brothers or sisters sometimes write to express worry about

their siblings' risky behaviors, such as substance abuse or cutting. As in prior years, many only children say that they are envious of friends with siblings.

Another common topic in our conversations with kids is stepfamilies. Kids frequently write to us about the adjustments required to make room for stepparents, stepsiblings, and half-siblings, but blended families are so common that they no longer come with a stigma. Sadly, kids with LGBTQ parents often need help facing criticism, ridicule, or even contempt, as do kids with parents of different races.

Grandparents continue to be enormous influences in the lives of children and are more likely today to head households with kids. But even when they are not the guardians, they are frequently the go-to relative when a child needs unhurried time and attention or needs to feel a little unconditional love.

> Family leaves an indelible impression on a child. Kids are always watching the adults around them and learning, even when we wish they were not.

Family leaves an indelible impression on a child. Kids are always watching the adults around them and learning, even when we wish they were not. Occasionally, readers write to us about some deeply distressing experience. Almost always, these childhood traumas are a by-product of adult problems, such as domestic violence, substance abuse, parental fighting, and acrimonious divorce. Some of the traumas are a result of circumstances beyond control, such as a serious illness or the death of a parent. Children, of course, navigate difficult circumstances differently. Many children are resilient, while for others the effects of these difficulties are rarely completely overcome. When we reply to letters from these kids, we work hard to make sure they feel heard and supported. We reassure them that they are not responsible for what has happened and urge them not to take on blame. Often, our message is that they are not alone. We strongly encourage them to share their feelings with trusted adults in their circle who, we hope, can better gauge the need for professional mental-health treatment.

Family dynamics and structure change throughout life, as do roles. Ideas about what constitutes a good family situation and a happy childhood have changed over the years and are still debated today. But what cannot be debated are the stabilizing, basic building blocks of family—love and trust. Arguably, one of the best ways we help most of our readers is by reminding them that family life is often imperfect and that the ways family members express interest and concern are sometimes flawed—but the love is there, and it endures.

Our hope for children everywhere is that childhood—a short, critically important season of life—will be nurturing, distinguished by family relationships that are warm, responsive, and predictably stable. This is the kind of support all children need to thrive, feel safe to explore the world, and engage positively with others. An attentive, caring family, however it is configured, puts kids solidly on the path to becoming their best selves.

It is me again,
I have another problem, all of my
friends have a sibling except for
one but I never get to see her,
I have no syblings at all, And my
Bestest froend ever has a
baby sisten and it is all about
he baby sister. P.S. I hope you can
put this in the book, (I Love your highlight)

me

—Savannah, 2014

Dear Highlights,
I don't have any bothers or sisters and I get bored and lonesome and I get tired of doing the same old thing. Please help!

—Chrissy, age 10, 1985

Dear Savannah,

Your drawing lets us know how sad this situation makes you feel. It might help you to know that other kids have written to us about feeling sad because they don't have any brothers and sisters.

We suggest that you find other ways to satisfy your desire to be with younger children. Maybe you could ask your best friend if you could sometimes play with and help take care of her baby sister, as long as it's OK with her parents. Do you have some relatives who have a baby in the family whom you could play with and help to take care of? We're sure the parents would appreciate your help.

A big part of growing up is learning to accept a situation the way it is and choosing to make the best of it. We can't always have what we want, but we can still choose to be happy!

We hope this helps.

Dear Highlights,
I like biking, but I have a big family that consists of 2 parents, me-9, my brothers-6, 5 & 3. We're almost always busy, and we just almost never have time.

—Anonymous, age 9, 2013

Dear Friend,

You are very fortunate to have such a big family, but we can understand how this would make it hard to find biking time. We encourage you to sit down with your parents and talk about this question. Explain in a calm, clear way that you really enjoy bike riding and you're looking for more times when you can pursue this interest. Make sure they know that you understand how busy your family is and that you are willing to work around the family's schedule. Then, listen well to what they have to say. We believe they will have some good suggestions for you.

Here are a few ideas that may help. Perhaps you and your family can make a schedule, writing in the many commitments and activities going on for everyone and then finding free times that could be used for biking. Setting specific time aside will make it easier to plan for it. If it's too difficult to find a time when everyone is free to bike, you could ask your parents about biking with friends or relatives. Depending on the layout and safety of your neighborhood, you might even talk to your parents about places you can bike without an adult riding with you, such as your driveway or up and down your street. Of course, it is your parents' decision, and it is their job to keep you safe. Respect their wishes regarding safety—especially about the times and places you can ride.

Remember, even if you aren't able to bike as much as you want to, think of other activities—running, climbing, jumping rope, etc. They are great muscle-strengthening exercises that will come in handy next time you're on a bike.

Dear Highlights,

My Mom and my Grandma said "Don't cross the street and go to where is my friends are." But I allway get so angry from them. I'm 9 years old and I know to cross the street. can you help please?

—Brianna, age 9, 2013

Dear Brianna,

We hope you will realize that your mom and your grandma have said this because they are concerned for your safety. Although you know how to cross the street, accidents do happen, and they can happen even when people are being careful. They don't want you to be hurt by a car or some other vehicle.

Try to explain to your mom and grandma how you are feeling—but don't get angry. Anger rarely solves anything, and it can make it harder to find solutions. If you can show them that you are mature and able to take care of yourself, perhaps they will be willing to let you cross the street on your own. If not, we hope you will be able to accept their decision. Be patient—we're sure the day will come when you will be able to cross the street on your own!

Dear Highlights,
My mom is always on her phone. I always ask her to get off, but she doesn't. She's on it half the day, and the other half she's working. All I want to do is spend time with her more. What should I do?

—Anonymous, 2020

Dear Friend,

We encourage you to talk with your mom about this. You could ask her to set aside specific time to talk so that she knows you'd like a serious conversation without distractions. You might start with something such as, "I love you, Mom, but I feel bad when we don't spend much time together. I know you work a lot and I appreciate that, but I would like to spend more time with you. Could we talk about it?" You might suggest simply spending some time together talking about what each of you did during the day. You could try making it a daily routine that the two of you talk for five or ten minutes after dinner or before bedtime.

Whether or not your mom agrees to make any changes, you can still make some changes on your own. You might try purposefully being near your mom and participating in what she's doing. For instance, have you considered sharing more household chores with her? Folding laundry, washing dishes, or preparing meals can be a good time to talk, sing, or tell jokes. Another thing to try is to schedule time to do things together. For example, you could both decide that at 7:00 on Friday nights you'll play games together for an hour. We're sure that you and your mom can come up with other good ideas.

Smiles, a good attitude, and a real desire to let your mom know she is important to you can make a huge difference. If one idea doesn't work, don't let yourself become discouraged or give up. Just try another approach!

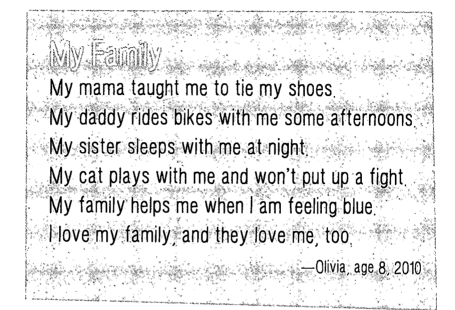

My Family

My mama taught me to tie my shoes.
My daddy rides bikes with me some afternoons.
My sister sleeps with me at night.
My cat plays with me and won't put up a fight.
My family helps me when I am feeling blue.
I love my family, and they love me, too.

—Olivia, age 8, 2010

—Erinne, age 6, 1993

Dear Highlights,
I really want a dog, but my mom is allegic to all mammals. (Except humans) and I don't want a fish. What should I do?

—Amber, age 10, 2017

Dear Amber,

We're glad you wrote to us. Having an allergy like that must be difficult for your mom.

Many people enjoy different kinds of reptiles. We don't know how you and other family members feel about this, but it's something to consider. If you have a chance to visit a pet store, you might get some other ideas for a pet besides fish. Fish are graceful and fascinating, but we understand that you can't cuddle and get close to them as you would a dog!

It may seem that you will have to wait until you are out on your own to have a pet. That may seem too long of a wait, but there are times when we all have to accept a situation for what it is. We encourage you to focus your thoughts and energy on the many things in your life that make you happy rather than on what you can't have. Don't let your happiness depend upon having a dog. You can make the most of every day with or without a pet.

Dear Highlights,
I need some advice. Star Wars has taken over my kid sister's mind. How can I convince her that sometimes I have other things on my mind?

—Katie, 1979

Dear Katie,

We think we know what you mean. Your sister thinks about *Star Wars* and talks about it all the time.

Don't worry. Just be patient and wait for your sister to lose her interest in *Star Wars*. Believe it or not, this will happen. In the meantime, you will just have to live with it.

Dear Highlights,
My mother and father divorced when I was a baby. Four months ago my father had a baby with his wife. Now my mother is pregnant. I feel like nobodys gonna care about me anymore.
P.S. What can I do?

–Sierra, 2015

Dear Sierra,

It may help to know that many older siblings feel this way when a baby is born in their family. Suddenly, the attention shifts from being just on you to being on you and your new sibling. This isn't a bad thing; it's just an adjustment. We promise you that your parents have not forgotten about you or stopped loving you. Their love has just expanded to make room for you and your new siblings.

It may help to let your parents know how you are feeling. It's important for them to know that you worry about feeling neglected. This way, they will know how to help you feel included and loved.

A baby is an exciting addition to a family, but it's also one that requires a lot of work. Your parents may seem more tired now than they were before, and they may ask you to help out with the babies. We hope you will have an open mind and be willing to help when needed (or volunteer even if no one asks you directly for help). Your parents will appreciate your willingness to lend a hand.

Congratulations on being an older sister! We know you will be a great example for your siblings.

Dear Highlights,
I have a stepdad. Whenever I ask him a question, he asks a question back. I don't like it. And my stepmom is always reading, and she doesn't seem to like me.

—Kathy, 1987

Dear Kathy,

Whenever stepfamilies are formed, it takes a while for everyone to get used to each other's different personalities and ways of doing things. We are sure that both your stepmom and your stepdad do like you and want to get along well with you. Do your best to accept them as they are, and we expect that they will do the same. As you come to know each other better, you will discover that the things which used to bother you are small in comparison to the whole person.

Learning to live in a stepfamily takes time, Kathy. If you give it your best effort, we think things will work out just fine.

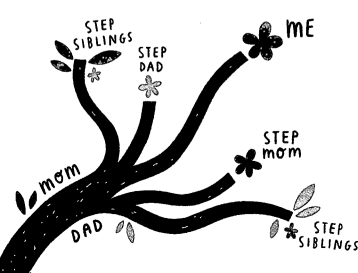

Dear Highlights,
My mom and dad have been separated for about a month. Now my dad wants to come back. I'm not sure I want him back.

—K. D., 1991

Dear K. D.,

Your feelings are normal. You have been on a kind of emotional roller coaster, feeling lots of ups and downs. Things probably settled down after your dad had been gone awhile, and now you're afraid of what might happen when he returns. But try to accept your dad again as part of your family. It's up to your mom and dad to work things out, but your attitude is important, too. Concentrate on your dad's good qualities and give him credit for wanting to come back. No matter what happens between your mom and your dad, remember that each of them loves you.

Dear Highlights,

I live with my grandma, 2 uncles, my cousin, and my dog. My grandma has custody of me. I told my grandma that I want to live with my mom, but she told me no and I'll never live with her. My mom visits me every day and buys me my clothing, she buys me food, and everything I need while my grandma doesn't buy me those things. My grandma said I'm never living with my mom. I want to live with my mom but my grandma won't let me. What should I do?

—Anonymous, 2016

Dear Friend,

You might try discussing your concern with your grandma when both of you are in a good mood. You could start by telling her how much you love and appreciate her. Then you can explain how you feel. In the conversation, it may help to use "I" sentences rather than "you" sentences. For example, instead of saying, "You don't let me live with Mom, and that's not fair," you could say, "I would like to understand better why I can't live with my mom. Can we talk about it?" Starting with "I" rather than "you" can set a gentler, less blaming tone. After you've spoken, you can give your grandma time to talk, without interrupting.

Your grandma may have reasons for her decision that she doesn't feel comfortable sharing with you. Try to respect this. For now, you may have to accept that you can see your mom, but not live with her. Perhaps you can be thankful that you get to see her regularly.

Make the most of your time with her. We know the situation is not exactly the way you want it to be, but life can certainly be good even if it's not perfect.

When you find yourself getting upset, it could help to take a few slow, deep breaths and slowly count to ten in your head. As you count, think of a peaceful image, such as your favorite place. It can also help to express your feelings with writing, drawing, or other creative activities. Listening to music, taking your dog for a walk, reading, or playing with friends can help make you feel better.

You might also share your feelings with another trusted adult. Many kids find it helpful to confide in a school counselor. Part of his or her job is to listen to kids' concerns and to offer guidance about things going on at school or at home. Other people you may feel comfortable talking to might include a teacher or the parent of a close friend.

I'll Be Mad

If my brother knocks over my tower of blocks
I'll be madder than Mommy when he breaks something
I'll be madder than the sky in a thunderstorm
I'll be madder than a tree when it falls down
I'll be madder than flowers in a rainstorm
I'll be madder than the ocean when the waves get high
I'll be madder than a ship when it sinks
I'll be mad as mad can be
   But I'll forgive him.

—Katie, age 6, 2000

—Gabrielle, age 4, 2002

Dear Highlights,
My mom and grandmother don't like me to read science fiction books, such as Animorphs. I try to collect them, but they won't let me buy any more. They said I won't learn anything from them. Should I quit reading Animorphs?

—Scott, 2000

Dear Scott,

You might try to explain to your mom what you think you gain by reading these books. For example, since a lot of kids read and collect such books, many of them make new friends by talking about the books with their classmates. Perhaps you could reach a compromise in which you agree to read one or two books that are not science fiction for each Animorphs book you read. Regardless of what you and your mom decide what is best for you, you must respect her decision. Keep in mind that there are many excellent books, full of adventure, that are not science fiction. Your librarian can help you find some.

Dear Highlights,
my brother used his wits to construct a toy lightsaber that he is best at dueling with, one that he can even finally beat me from time to time. Instead of being angry or enraged, i feel... happy... proud. I don't know how to interpret this. can you help me out, here, Highlights?

—Anonymous, 2020

Dear Friend,

We're so glad to hear that you're proud of your brother for constructing his toy lightsaber. We understand why your feelings could be confusing—but they are good feelings! The pride and happiness that you feel is probably a result of watching him improve. Have you been teaching him or giving him tips? Have the two of you spent a lot of time practicing together? No doubt your brother is proud of himself, too. Younger siblings often look up to older siblings, and being able to defeat you in play fighting is a big milestone for him. You are watching him grow up, little by little, and because you have been a key player in this part of his childhood, you can share in his happiness. We hope you and your brother continue to bond—over light-sabers or anything else—for a long time.

Dear Highlights,
I have two older sisters.
Sometimes they play
games and don't ask me
to play. One of them has
a car. When I ask if I can
go to the store with her,
she says no. What can
I do?

—Stephanie, 1982

Dear Stephanie,

Your problem is not unusual. Each person in a family needs some time to herself. Your sisters do not always want to take you along with them. That does not mean that they do not love you very much. We think, as you all get older, you will understand that. Try to talk to your sisters and tell them how much you enjoy being with them. But try also to understand that sometimes they like to do things alone.

Dear Highlights,
I am going to have a baby brother or sister, and everyone tells me that it will be annoying. What should I do?

—Daneasha, 2005

Dear Daneasha,

Try talking to your parents about this. They will be able to give you an idea of what to expect when the baby is born. There may be things you can do to help welcome the new baby, such as sorting baby clothes or helping fix up the baby's room. Being involved in the preparations may help you feel less worried about what it will be like when he or she arrives. Being a big sister can be a wonderful experience. Just because others tell you that the baby will be annoying doesn't mean they are right. If you have a positive attitude, you may find you enjoy having a new baby in the house.

Sisterhood

Having a sister is a real treat,
especially when you tickle her feet.

You watch her laugh and watch her cry,
you even watch her childhood go by.

You play together, even fight,
but still you love her with all your might.

She may be mean sometimes, it's true,
but deep inside, she looks up to you.

She makes you happy, she makes you glad
to say "You're the best I've ever had!"

—Allie, age 11, 2017

—Mary Ann, age 4, 1960

Dear Highlights,

I am the eldest in a family of five children, and in the 9th grade. I try to help my siblings as their big sister, but now have a dilemma. We will be adopting a little child soon, and the child shall be homeschooled with us. We have to go to classes and our homeschooling Group all week, and we all have had some problems with a few kids. They have been known to taunt these brothers and have directed racial slurs to my siblings. We are a biracial family and will become even more so after the adoption. Although some teasers have been rebuked, we can't completely control it. My question is, how can I be a supportive big sister and help my new sibling in a multiracial family? I am researching all I can but am having a hard time finding information on being supportive siblings.

—Ashley, 2011

Dear Ashley,

When readers write to us about teasing and bullying, we usually suggest that the best response is to completely ignore the people who are doing it. It is sad that these people don't know how to treat others with respect and kindness, but that behavior reflects on them, not on you or your siblings.

Usually, such people are trying to get a reaction. The more you react, the more satisfying it is to them. However, if there is ever any danger that you or your siblings will be hurt physically, an adult needs to know about that right away.

We encourage you and your siblings to stick together, and stick up for one another, so that none of you ever feels alone. If one of your siblings is being teased, another could put his or her arm around their shoulders. Then, they could simply walk away together without saying anything. Kids are less likely to tease people who stick together.

You mentioned that the teasers have been rebuked, so it seems that adults at the homeschool group know what's going on. Be sure to keep them posted. It's their job to keep the school safe and comfortable for all students. Perhaps your parents would agree to go with you to talk to them. Instead of focusing on punishing the teasers, which might not bring positive results, you might discuss the need to create a climate of friendship and tolerance in your homeschool group. Here's a website that may give you and your teachers ideas on positive things that can be done to oppose racism in schools and communities: tolerance.org. Always ask your parents for permission before going to a website you don't know.

Your siblings are fortunate to have someone like you to look out for them.

Dear Highlights,
My Mom and Dad always put up pictures of my brother and sister but barely any of mine. I am the middle child is it true that the middle child is overlooked? What do I do?

—Jada, 2014

Dear Jada,

We don't believe that middle children are overlooked by their parents on purpose, but we do believe that sometimes it may feel that way. We're certain, however, that your parents don't mean to have you feel left out.

We encourage you to talk to them about this. Try explaining how you feel sad and left out when you see the pictures of your siblings up but not many pictures of you. They love you very much and want you to be happy. We believe that they will be glad you confided in them.

Dear Highlights,
I have a twin sister, and everyone always compares us. How can I be seen for who I am without being compared to my sister?

—Melody, 1996

Dear Melody,

Twins can have remarkable similarities. These people may be trying to learn more about twins or simply making conversation.

When people compare the two of you, politely point out that you each have your own personalities and gifts. If they note similarities between you, take that opportunity to point out differences as well. And if someone compliments your sister, you can smile and say, "Yes, she's good at that." Be happy for her accomplishments, but realize that your abilities and purpose in life are just as important.

—Emily, age 10, 2019

Two Homes

I have two homes.
Most people have one home,
 but I have two.
My dad's house is scented with
 the wonderful smells from
 the food that he cooks.
My mom's house is small,
 warm, and cozy.
When I think of home, I think
 of two places.
I love both homes.
When I think of home, I think
 of two faces.

—Isabella, age 9, 2002

Dear ~~Highlights~~, My parents are lesbiah

I know it's okay to be difrent but I still Feel a bit weird about it

What do I do?!?!

—Thea, age 8, 2011

Dear Thea,

We hear from many kids who worry that their families are different in one way or another. Try to remember that every family is unique in its own way. These different family experiences are part of what makes the world interesting and beautiful. What's important is that your parents love you and provide you with a safe home.

We're sure your parents would like to know what's on your mind. When they're not too busy or tired to talk, let them know about your concerns. Remember to be respectful and kind and to listen carefully to what they have to say.

We're glad you wrote to us. Writing in a journal and doing artwork are other good ways to express some of the feelings you have.

Dear Highlights,

I beg my grandma to let me have the latest phone because they say the monthly bill will be high. How can I get an Android?

—Haley, 2013

Dear Haley,

We know that it's becoming more and more common for young people to have their own cell phones. However, at this time, it is more of a status symbol than an actual need for them to have one. There are certain situations in which it may be necessary for someone your age to have a cell phone. But for the most part, kids simply want one because others have them and can talk to or text their friends and play games at any time.

As you mentioned, the monthly bills can be high. In addition, phones are often stolen, lost, or misused. Unfortunately, not all the people who have them are using them wisely or responsibly.

We encourage you to respect your parents' and grandparents' wishes. If they feel it's not necessary for you to have a cell phone at this time, then we encourage you to accept their decision. They know what is best for you as well as what is possible for them. Begging your grandma for a phone may make her feel uncomfortable, so we suggest that you not put her in that position.

We hope this helps.

Dear Highlights,
Sometimes I feel that my parents care more about my brother than about me. My brother has a learning disability. So my parents say he needs special care, but how can I get them to understand that I need more love?

—Amanda, 1986

Dear Amanda,

We know that it can be difficult when a sister or brother has a disability. It does seem sometimes as though that youngster gets more than a fair share of attention. Because your brother has a learning disability rather than a more obvious handicap, it is even harder to understand sometimes why he deserves all this special treatment.

Because learning comes more easily to you, your parents don't need to give you so much extra help. That doesn't mean that they love you any less than they love your brother, though. The next time you talk to your parents, try not to make comparisons between you and your brother. Just tell your parents something like, "I wish we had more time to do things together." If you try to work with your parents instead of competing against your brother for their time, things will probably work out better for everyone.

My Father in Africa

My father is in Africa, far, far away.
I don't get to see him
As you see your father every day.
I love him, I miss him,
Even though he might be well or ill,
      I'll never know.
My father is in Africa, so very far away.
I wish I could be with him
Each minute of the day.

—Mona, age 9, 1964

—Eve, age 10

My Mother

My mother says she doesn't care
About the color of my hair,
Or if my eyes are blue or brown
Or if my nose turns up or down.
It really doesn't matter.

But if I cheat or tell a lie,
And do mean things to make folks cry,
And do not try to do what's right;
Then that does really matter.

It's not one's looks that make one great;
It's character that seals your fate.
It's what's within your heart, you see,
That makes or mars your destiny.

—Teresa, age 12, 1970

—Janice, age 7, 1948

Dear Highlights,
I'm going vegetarian, have been for almost a month, and my parents don't approve. They're almost trying to force me to eat meat. What do I do?

—Anonymous, 2014

Dear Friend,

Maybe it would help to have a calm conversation with your parents about your choice. Rather than trying to change their minds, you could ask them for the reasons why they disapprove of your vegetarianism. Perhaps they're worried that you won't get enough iron and protein in your diet. If this is the case, you could make a plan to research non-meat sources of these nutrients. If they are worried about planning special, vegetarian meals for you, you might offer to pitch in with cooking. By politely addressing your parents' concerns, you may be able to reach an understanding.

It may take time to see eye-to-eye with your parents, but we hope you'll remain patient. You may also want to let them know that you respect their decision to eat meat, even though you're taking a different path.

Dear Highlights,
Sometimes my mom and I disagree on things, then when I try to ask her a question she won't let me say what I want to say. She's the only one who gets to talk.

—Z. J., 1996

Dear Z. J.,

Perhaps sometime when the two of you are getting along and you both have time, you can talk about this. (If this doesn't work, try writing how you feel in a letter.) Calmly say how you feel and ask if you both might agree to some rules for future discussions. For example, you could agree that when one person is speaking, the other won't interrupt. Each person could hold up their hand when they "have the floor." When they put down their hand, the other person says in their own words what the first just said. Then the second person has their own turn to talk. This makes sure that you're each listening carefully and trying to understand. Not losing your temper can take practice, so stick with it.

Dear Highlights,
My little brother is always bugging me. Sometimes I can't even take it. Every time I start to play with something, he takes it away. My mom yells at me instead of him. Now I don't know what to do. Can you help me?

—Daniel, 1984

Dear Daniel,

Probably your mother yells at you because she knows you are more grown-up than your brother and ought to be able to figure out a way not to fight. First, think about why your little brother always wants to do whatever you are doing. It is because he looks up to you. He thinks you're pretty grown-up, too, and he wants to be just like you.

Try to find some time each day to spend just with him. If he knows that he can count on some special time of his own with you, he may be more willing to leave you alone when you want to play by yourself or with your friends. Also, if he thinks of you as his special friend, he won't want to make you mad by bugging you. We doubt that you will be able to stop fighting with your brother completely. Most brothers fight some. You can start to be friends with him now, and as you both get older, you may realize that you hardly fight at all anymore.

Dear Highlights,
My dad works during the night and I miss him all the time.
—P. J., 1998

Dear P. J.,

Parents have to do what they can to take care of their families. In your family, right now it means having your dad work at night. Parents don't always get to choose which hours they work—usually the company they work for assigns the schedule. It may be hard for your dad to work nights, but he wants to take good care of his family.

You might write notes to your dad. You could stick one in his jacket or pants pocket and tell him to read it at work. Ask him to write some notes to you and leave them at home for you to read while he's at work. He might even hide them around the house for you to find. If you and your dad set a certain time to read the other's note, you'll know that you'll both be reading about each other at the same time.

When your dad is home, you might offer to help him with chores. That way, you'll be spending time together. You can feel good about being his helper. Then he might have more free time to spend with you. You can also help your dad by being quiet during those times when he's sleeping. That can show him that you love and care about him.

Dear Highlights, My mom goes to Washington DC sometimes for 5 days, and I really miss her.

—Melody, age 7, 2020

Letters About School

SCHOOL IS SO EMBEDDED IN A CHILD'S LIFE THAT it is almost synonymous with childhood. Of course, learning happens at every turn and in all kinds of "classrooms"—home, camps, museums, virtual classrooms, the soccer field and dance studio, and even the backyard or playground. But most U.S. children will spend about a third of their days until age 18 in a classroom at a public or private school.

Many parents give school high priority, understanding that children's academic success matters and doing all they can to ensure positive outcomes. But the letters and emails Highlights receives from children remind us that kids are doing more in school than acquiring basic skills and knowledge. Not only are they learning about the world, but they are also learning about themselves and their place in the world.

Today, school gets serious fast beginning in kindergarten. For many children, it's a big leap to leave the familiarity and comfort of home, daycare, or preschool to begin formal schooling. Their new experience in a larger, highly structured environment outside the family can be unsettling. They are transitioning from the security and privilege of home, where they were made to feel uniquely special, to a classroom full of peers. In 1986, six-year-old Genevieve laid out some of the many challenges in her letter to us. "I have a new school and I'm not used to it," she wrote. "I'm afraid my first-grade class won't have enough for me to do. And I'm afraid the aids in the lunch room are mean . . . and I only know one kid and I don't know what to do."

For kids, finding their place and feeling a sense of belonging in school can be one of the biggest adjustments in childhood.

For kids, finding their place and feeling a sense of belonging in school can be one of the biggest adjustments in childhood. School is where first friendships are forged, where

they learn self-control, develop empathy, and learn to "play well with others." It's where, sometimes for the first time, kids must create a trusting relationship with a new kind of non-family authority figure—their teacher. It is where their worldview is expanded, and they begin to discover their own interests, capabilities, and personal challenges.

School plays such an important influence and places so many demands on children that it is little wonder kids need all the nurturing support we adults can give them. Over the decades, many children have looked to Highlights for that kind of support. In fact, school has consistently ranked among the top three topics kids write to us about (along with friendship and siblings).

The school environment has changed significantly from the days when kids walked to neighborhood schools, stood before classroom blackboards, and vied for the "fun" chore of clapping dusty erasers outdoors.

The school environment has changed significantly from the days when kids walked to neighborhood schools, stood before classroom blackboards, and vied for the "fun" chore of clapping dusty erasers outdoors. Yet the letters from kids about school have changed remarkably little. Kids still write to us about study habits, fear of speaking in front of the class, and test anxiety. They still request advice about getting along with classmates and dealing with pressure from parents to excel in school and extracurricular activities.

Sometimes, kids share drawings that reflect school pride or admiration for their teachers. They send letters expressing ongoing curiosity about the subjects they are studying. Often, the thoughts they share mirror the concerns of their parents—and this is where we most see modern times reflected. When standardized testing became high stakes, for example, we saw an increase in letters and emails about school stress. After the Sandy Hook Elementary School shooting in Newtown, Connecticut, we heard from children worried about their own safety in the classroom. In the spring of 2020, when COVID-19 forced the early closing of most U.S. schools and left kids wondering what the new school year in the fall would look like, many kids wrote to say how much they missed the social interactions school provided. Not only did they miss their friends, but they also seemed to miss the routine and intellectual stimulation of school. In their letters to us about being quarantined, kids were more likely to describe themselves as bored rather than worried or scared.

> When we write kids back, we do more than address their immediate concerns. We take the opportunity to share bigger ideas that we hope will help kids value education.

When we write kids back, we do more than address their immediate concerns. We take the opportunity to share bigger ideas that we hope will help kids value education. We want them to know that, yes, learning can be hard—but the hard things are often the things most worth doing. We try to help them see that the obstacles they face in the moment, such as struggling with math concepts, rarely translate into lifelong deficits if they continue to work hard to learn. Sometimes, the real obstacle is fear of failure and humiliation. That was certainly the case for George, who wrote in 1991, "Kids think I'm stupid. The more they say that, the more I believe them." We want kids to know that making mistakes is a core part of learning for all of us, that asking questions in school is not only a good idea but it's also encouraged, and that it's OK to look for help when you need it.

Whether kids write to us about their failure to live up to their parents' or teachers' expectations (or their own), pressure from peers, or their feelings of being a school outsider, we try to praise effort, offer plenty of reassurance, and express optimism that it will all get better. We want kids to shed any feelings of shame, fear, or humiliation, as these emotions only fuel school apathy.

Although the kids who write to us may be too young to take the long view, we hope to help kids (and their parents) see that doing well in school is about more than earning good grades. We hope that, over time and as kids grow, they'll see that knowledge is empowering, and that school done well helps them grow into people who understand their own strengths, work well with others, cope with real problems, and grow up confident. So, in our conversations with readers about school, we say in various ways, "Kid, you've got this."

Dear Highlights

I am Scared to enter
Middle school because I won't
Know any one. All the other
Kids have been together since
Kindergarden. How can I
not be as scared as I am
now?

—Mason, age 10, 2015

Dear Highlights,

I am 12 and going to a Middle School. I am excited to go because there would be more kids like me, but there are other things I'm afraid of. Like kids will make fun of my name, I'm proud of it, but there are alot of kids who care alot about the races. Also, I'm a good student an A, I'm afraid kids will make fun of me. Call me goody 2 shoes. Also, I had trouble with friends at the Elementary school and afraid I won't have any friends to hang out with there. I really want a best friend. I am really nervous. What if I can't get the work done. Please help me!

—Jin-ho, age 12, 1999

Dear Jin-ho,

We're glad to hear that you're proud of your name, Jin-ho. Although it's true that some kids may tease you, try to remember that others won't. Try to set an example of how people should treat others. Treat everyone as you would have them treat you. A person will often tease if they know it will make someone upset. If a student picks on you, ignore their comments. Walk away or concentrate on your work. Once they realize that you won't react to teasing, they may stop bothering you. If it continues, then you might want to talk with an adult you trust, perhaps a parent or a teacher.

It's true that you may have more homework in middle school, and you might have to study harder. One key to doing well in school is organization. Maybe you can use a calendar to keep track of your assignments and activities. You could set up a time after school when you will always do your homework. Try establishing good study habits at the beginning of the school year.

You mentioned that you are worried about having friends during middle school. Give yourself a chance to meet new people. Friendships take time to develop. Try talking to one new person every day, whether it's in class or during lunch. Try joining clubs, sports teams, or other groups that interest you. Then you'll have many opportunities to meet lots of new people and find new friends.

Try not to worry about things that might not happen. Many of your fellow students are probably having the same questions and concerns. Middle school is a change from elementary school, and you're right to be excited. We're glad that you want middle school to be a good experience.

Dear Highlights,
I have a problem. How am I going to get to play outside? I have so many things to do when I come home from school. I get out at 3:00 and sometimes after school the girls play basketball in our gym. One night a week I go to band and don't get home until 4:30. Two nights a week I have sports. I also have a lot of homework and I have to practice my instrument.

—Jane, 1968

Dear Highlights,
I've been getting so much homework that I barely have time to play. What should I do?

—Destiny, 2016

Dear Destiny,

To give yourself the most time to play, it's important to use your time wisely. If you're given time to do your homework during school hours, try your best to finish as much as you can. Then, as soon as you get home from school, start the rest of your homework. Perhaps you can break it up into two parts. In between, give yourself a 30-minute break to play. If you concentrate hard, you might be surprised at how quickly you can finish your work. Once you're done, you'll be able to enjoy a feeling of freedom for the rest of the evening. If you're still feeling overwhelmed, talk to your parents and teachers for their suggestions.

My Third-Grade Teacher, Mrs. Williams

My favorite teacher is
  Mrs. Williams.
She taught me to reach for
  the stars.
And now I think someday
I might like to visit Mars.
So thank you,
Mrs. Williams,
for all you have done.
You make learning
so much fun.

—Elijah, age 8, 2010

—Briani, age 10, 2003

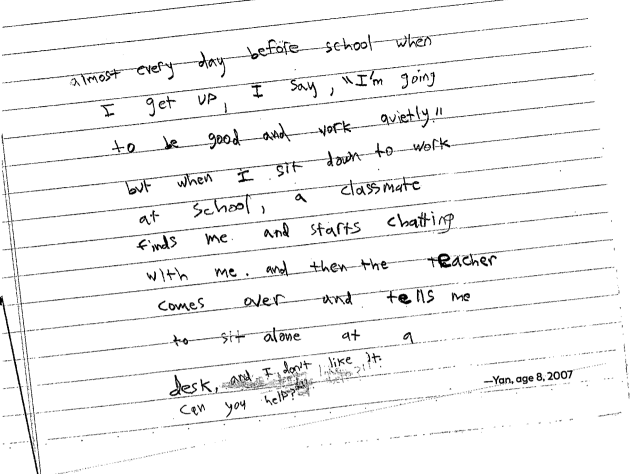

almost every day before school when I get up, I say, "I'm going to be good and work quietly." but when I sit down to work at school, a classmate finds me and starts chatting with me. and then the teacher comes over and tells me to sit alone at a desk, and I don't like it. Can you help?

—Yan, age 8, 2007

Dear Yan,

Have you tried talking to your parents about this? If you explain to them how hard you are trying, they might be able to offer you some great suggestions. It might also be a good idea to talk to your teacher. They would probably be happy to know how you feel. We bet your teacher has encountered students with similar difficulties in the past and would be able to offer some good advice.

If you find that the same two or three classmates keep interrupting your work, you may want to explain to them what is happening. Tell them you don't like having to sit alone at your desk, and you would appreciate it if they wouldn't talk to you while you are working quietly. Then, if someone begins to interrupt you during class time, they will know what's going on if you simply point to your work or whisper, "I can't talk."

Good luck. If you stay determined to focus on your schoolwork, you will be able to do it.

Dear Highlights,
I want to be in the CHESS
CLUB at my school, but lots
of people think that CHESS
is for dorks and I don't want
my friends to think I'm a
dork. Can you help me?

—Ivy, 1998

Dear Ivy,

We all have different likes and dislikes.
That's what makes each of us unique.
Chess is a strategic game and takes
patience and thinking skills. Sometimes
people make fun of the interests of
others because they don't understand
these interests. They might think it covers
up their ignorance by teasing others.

It takes courage to step out and do
something different from your friends.
Part of growing up is choosing to do
things that best suit your interests,
whether or not other people approve of
them. Each of us has special talents to
cultivate. To waste them because of other
people's thoughts would be a shame.

Stepping out and fulfilling your
heart's desire could encourage your
friends to look for their own unique
talents. It takes confidence to pursue a
special interest. Be proud of who you are.

Dear Highlights,
Everybody says my fifth-
grade teacher is going to be
strict. What should I do?

—Clint, 1996

Dear Clint,

Wait until you have this teacher,
then judge for yourself. Your
opinion may be different from
your friends'. Teachers, like parents
and friends, have different styles
and personalities. Try to remember
that learning to get along with all
kinds of people is a valuable skill.
And you may find that a strict
teacher runs an orderly and fair
class in which you can learn a lot.
Most teachers just want you to
listen, do your best, follow rules,
and be respectful of others.

Dear Highlights,
I don't like math but my parents tell me to do it almost every day! Can you help me understand why it's important?

—Isabelle, 2012

Dear Isabelle,

Some subjects will be helpful to a person's career someday, but all subjects can make everyday life better.

Can you see how you'd use math in these everyday situations? Ordering pizzas for a group; making time to play and do homework; figuring out sports statistics; deciding how much money to take on a field trip; making half a recipe; and doing woodwork or crafts. Try to find math throughout your day. You'll see it everywhere. You may not enjoy practicing it, but you'll be glad you did when you need to use it.

Dear Highlights,
I have a problem getting along with teachers. They keep on telling me too many things to do. What should I do to get along with them?

—Joshua, 1988

Dear Joshua,

A good talk with one of your teachers is the most direct way to tackle the problem. It might also help to have a talk with your mom, your dad, or some other adult. They may have some good advice about how to get along better with your teachers.

Your teachers are probably doing what they feel is best for you. If they give you many things to do, it is most likely because they want you to learn many things and do your best. Try to write down your assignments and do them as well as you can.

Once your teachers see that you are working hard to try to get along better, things will probably change.

Forgot My Homework

Oh, I forgot my homework,
Oh, what a drag,
Oh, I forgot my homework,
I forgot to put it in my bookbag.

Oh, what should I do?
Oh, what should I say?
Should I tell my teacher
My little brother threw it away?

Although I should tell the truth,
I know I shouldn't lie,
I won't be able to talk very well,
For I'm getting ready to cry!

—Breanne, age 8, 2003

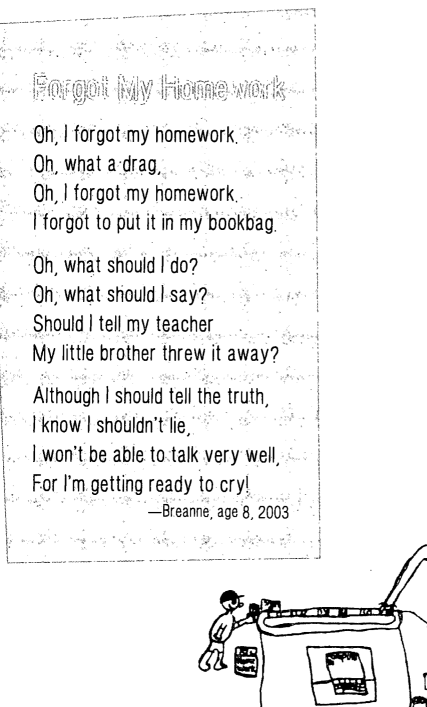

The Homework Machine
—Melissa, age 9, 1989

Age:9

At Shcool I had to do a lap around the grass. I seen a pine cone and I picked it up and trew it Then, It Bances off the ground and hits this guy in the back and I said Im sorry I did not mean it to hit you. And he said ya, right and told the teach and prinecapal and the teacher told my granurma becaus I live with her and I told her what happen and no one believes me. What do I do?

I really need your help on this one! :) P.S. I love your books they are awsome and in the december book in the Carft's can you teach us how to make a snow flacke? :)

—Brittany, age 9, 2013

Dear Brittany,

We're sorry that no one believes you when you say you didn't throw the pine cone at a boy on purpose. Sometimes we're just in the wrong place at the wrong time. We're proud of you for doing the right thing and apologizing to the boy, even though you didn't mean for the pine cone to hit him.

Instead of focusing on the negative outcome of this incident, try to put it behind you and save your energy for more important things. Sometimes no matter how hard we try, we just can't convince people of something. If you know you didn't hit the boy with a pine cone on purpose, then you should be able to reassure yourself that you know the truth and that's the most important thing.

Dear Highlights,
My sisters, brothers and I are home-schooled. A lot of people don't have a very high opinion of us. They think we can do whatever we want, but that's not true. We have a time to start school and a time to be done. I just want to inform your readers that home-schoolers aren't at home for their parents to baby them.

—Katie, 1995

Dear Katie,

It's easy to misjudge things we don't know about. And, just as classes are different in difficulty and in teaching style, homeschooling is, too. People who think it's easy may know someone who homeschools and doesn't have the rules you do. Try to be understanding when someone is uninformed. If you give information patiently and calmly, you'll have a better chance of your message getting through.

SCIENCE
ENGLISH
HISTORY
MATH

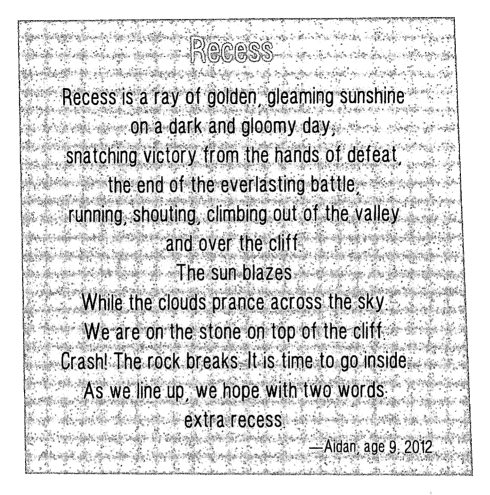

Recess

Recess is a ray of golden, gleaming sunshine
on a dark and gloomy day,
snatching victory from the hands of defeat,
the end of the everlasting battle,
running, shouting, climbing out of the valley
and over the cliff.
The sun blazes
While the clouds prance across the sky.
We are on the stone on top of the cliff.
Crash! The rock breaks. It is time to go inside.
As we line up, we hope with two words:
extra recess.

—Aidan, age 9, 2012

—Sonya, age 8, 1978

Dear Highlights,
In school, I am one of the unusually smarter kids. So in math, when the problems are really hard, the other kids are always asking me what the answers are, or they're telling me to do the work for them. Can you help me?

—Emma, age 11, 2007

Dear Emma,

It's great that you're such a good student, Emma. We understand it can put you in a difficult spot with your classmates. Although you might like to help them sometimes, you seem to realize that it's important that they do their own math. Also, it's not really fair for you to do the work and for them to get a "free ride."

We encourage you to talk with your teacher at a time when your classmates aren't around. Let your teacher know that you feel uncomfortable when others ask you for help on school-work that is meant to be completed independently. In a very respectful and calm voice, explain why this bothers you. You might ask the teacher to keep an eye on the students sitting around you the next time the class has an assignment that is not meant to be done as a group.

When your teacher assigns group work, we encourage you to do your best to help others. However, there is nothing wrong with politely refusing to give others answers when you know that they are supposed to be completing their work on their own, whether it's classwork or homework. If your teacher would like you to help your classmates sometimes, try to guide them in finding the answers instead of doing the work for them. Your teacher can give you tips on how to do this.

Fights at scool

Dear Highlights,
Evry day at scool
I always get in a fight
with sombody. And I only
feel like telling my mom
about the parts where I
get hurt, and she fixes me
up. Highlights what should
I do about my problems!

—Cody, 2000

Dear Cody,

It's great that you want to solve this problem. We suggest that you tell your mom more than the parts you feel like telling her. Even if you have to take some of the blame for fighting, you will have to face up to all of it before you can find a solution to your problems.

Think back over the last few fights you have had. We think you will see that in each case, you were not able to control what the other person did. You can only control what you do. If the other person picks a fight, that person will get a fight only if you agree to it.

If other kids are bullying you—or trying to bully you—then you should tell your mom about it right away. Bullying is serious and adults need to become involved to stop it. Remember that telling an adult is not "tattling" when someone is being hurt.

One thing you can do is learn how to control your temper. Many people say that they feel less angry if they walk away from the situation. Others stop what they are doing and slowly, silently, count to ten. Then they have more control over their anger and can react without fighting.

Dear Highlights,
I'm going to a new school and I don't know if it's safe and secure or not. Please help!
—Owen, age 12, 2019

Dear Owen,

If you haven't already, we encourage you to talk to your parents about this. They want you to feel safe and comfortable in your new school. You can also talk to a teacher and school counselor, who can reassure you that the adults at your school and others in your community work hard to be sure that everyone is safe.

Of course, if you notice that someone or something might pose a danger, it's important to report it. It's not tattling to protect someone from being hurt.

Dear Highlights,
My third grade class is doing swim safty lesons. All of the girls have to change in a locker room together and some of my friends are embaresd. What should I tell them.

—Hannah, age 8, 2012

Dear Hannah,

It is a perfectly natural response to be shy about undressing in front of other people. Everyone's body is beautiful, and we all come in different shapes and sizes. Everyone should respect one another and focus on what's important: swim safety and having fun. If a friend feels especially nervous, perhaps she can change in a bathroom stall. If any of the girls are unkind or not respectful, we suggest you speak to your mom or gym teacher about this.

Dear Highlights,

During this summer I went on vacation for 3 weeks, but the problem is, you see, I have to go to summer school. I'm having no fun and doing assignments most of the time. I believe that this contradicts the point of summer. Whenever I try to convince my parents to stop having me do this, they always say, "It's to prepare you for the next grade . . ." They won't even let me have a week off of the summer school! And whenever I do bad (get bad grades, etc) they get mad at me and I start to cry. The worse thing is, I have the same summer school as my after school! The last thing that makes this place so bad is that they teach us things that are way too hard!

—Jacob, 2017

Dear Jacob,

We hear from many kids who do not enjoy attending summer school. It can be difficult to focus on schoolwork when you feel as if the rest of your friends are having fun.

It may not feel this way right now, but summer school is one of the best ways to prepare yourself for the new school year. Each grade gets a little more difficult and attending summer school allows you to get a head start on the new material. This could be why the assignments feel more difficult than your homework last year.

Did you know that some schools never take summer vacations? These schools often take long breaks, but the students attend year-round. This is to help them remember what they've learned all year.

We encourage you to discuss your feelings about summer school with your parents. They will be able to explain their decision to you. They can also help you with your homework or help you talk with your teacher about ways to make things more manageable. We encourage you to talk to your teacher, too. Ask questions when you don't understand an assignment. The teacher is there to help you.

Dear Highlights,

I just started 4th grade and it's very hard for me. I have to keep up with my chrome book and charging it, and filling out my reading log, and many other things. Any Idies?

P.S. If you decide to put this in could you base the picture on this?

—Gabriella, age 9, 2017

Dear Gabriella,

We hope you will talk to your parents about this. Since they know you best, they will have helpful ideas. Your teacher can give you some good tips, too.

It might help to develop a schedule for yourself. For example, you could set a special time each day to charge your Chromebook and fill out your reading log, perhaps right after dinner each evening. Or choose a time that works best for you. Eventually, you will find that it has become a habit and you won't forget.

It's good to set a schedule for yourself because as you get older, you will have more responsibilities and are likely to be involved in more activities. We encourage you to write down everything you do during the week—school, homework, reading, family time, chores, extracurricular activities, time to exercise, time to relax, and spending time with friends. By making a plan, you will probably find that everything is a little easier. We hope you will talk to your parents as you develop a plan that works for your family.

Dear Highlights,
I am 10 years old. I would like to tell you about my school. We have a school government with a Governor and a Council. I ran for Governor two times and won once. When we run for Governor or Council, we have to make speeches and have a campaign. We have jobs like watering the plants, police officers, taking roll, and we get paid play money once a week for doing our job. If we talk when we shouldn't, we get fined. We even have savings bonds and checking accounts. When we have four hundred dollars, we can buy a chair anywhere in the room. You really learn about life and living with our government.
                    —Scott, age 10, 1968

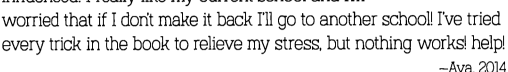

Dear Highlights,

I have this big national exam to take in about 2 weeks' time! The results will determine what secondary school I will be going to for the next 4 years. I don't want to be in a school that's badly influenced! I really like my current school and I'm worried that if I don't make it back I'll go to another school! I've tried every trick in the book to relieve my stress, but nothing works! help!

—Ava, 2014

Dear Ava,

The important thing to remember is that all any of us can do is our personal best. It's likely that after you take the test, you'll ask yourself why you were so worried!

After reviewing the material that you think may be on the test, quiz yourself or ask a family member or friend to quiz you to see if you know the material. That will help you see if there is more that you need to review before test time.

Get a good night's rest before the test. Wake up in time to have a nutritious breakfast, then go to school with a positive attitude. Believe it or not, your attitude can affect your performance on a test. If you are worried and dreading it, you are more likely to make mistakes than if you are confident and ready to

do your best. Remind yourself that you are well prepared. Then, focus on one question at a time and take time at the end to review your answers.

Breathing is a great way to calm yourself down. When you feel yourself stressing out or getting anxious, pause and take three long, deep breaths. Focus on the breath going in and out of your lungs and deep into your belly. You will immediately feel calmer.

Exercise is also a good way to combat stress. Go outside and play sports with friends or ride a bike. Also, focus on fun things to do: Make plans with friends, learn how to make a new food with your parents, play games with your siblings, or read a good book. If you keep your mind occupied with fun things, you may eventually feel the stress start to melt away.

Getting Ready for School

Get out your paper,
Get out your pencils,
Jump out of the pool,
And get ready for school.

Summer is over,
We've had lots of fun,
But we have to remember
That school is
NUMBER one!

—Kelly, age 8, 1997

—Betsy, age 8, 1990

Letters About Friendship

EVERY CHILD NEEDS AND WANTS FRIENDS. FRIENDS enrich our lives with fun, laughter, and camaraderie. But friends play an even bigger role in the lives of kids. Friends are an essential part of kids' social-emotional development—a vital part of growing up.

Friendship, like family, opens the door for kids to learn about themselves. By making and keeping friends, kids learn important life skills, such as getting along with others and resolving conflicts. Friendship offers kids a means of exploring identity and self-understanding. Positive interactions with friends build self-esteem and help kids feel a sense of belonging. Plus, all this benefits kids not only in childhood but also later in life. Successful childhood friendships correlate with successful adult relationships.

But friendship comes with expectations, and understanding these expectations is part of the important work of childhood. To make friends, kids must learn how to start a conversation and how to participate in the give-and-take of dialogue. When they hang out with friends, kids practice reading social cues and hearing different points of view. To keep friends, kids must learn to think of others and show that they can be trustworthy and kind, which isn't always easy. The world of friendship can be tricky to traverse, and every child, at some time in their childhood, needs help managing its inevitable peaks and valleys. In fact, *Highlights* receives more mail asking for advice about friendship than any other subject.

The children who write to us are aging out of the early stage of friendship, which is mostly about fun and playing with other kids who are conveniently at hand. Around the time they start elementary school, kids are more aware of the feelings of others and begin to appreciate the benefits of friendship. As kids grow, their friendships become less transactional and are instead built on shared interests, trust, kindness, empathy, and even gender. Developing a self-identity and being able to recognize true friendship is crucial as kids reach adolescence—the time when friends take on even deeper significance and kids often look more to peers for guidance and support.

The mail we receive tells us that the highs and lows of childhood friendship have changed very little over the decades. The conflicts kids describe may seem small and trivial to adults, but they can be powerful in their ability to rob kids of their confidence and sense of belonging. For decades, kids have written to us about the pain of being betrayed by a friend—of being put down with hurtful words or made to feel left out. In 1987, Amy wrote to say that the girl she thought was her best friend named someone else as her best friend. "My feelings are very hurt. She's the only girl I want to be best friends with. What should I do?" In 2015, Mckenzie told us about a friend who called her a "stupid idiot and other bad names," but then in school pretended it didn't happen. "What should I do?" she wondered.

The conflicts can leave kids confused about how they should feel. Should they take the blame? Should they feel shame? Should they stand up for themselves? In 1985, a Canadian reader wrote to say that she was always scared her friends might not like her ideas. "I am afraid that they might think my opinion is stupid. Can you give me some ideas to prevent that?"

Kids also write to us for help resisting peer pressure. Some have written about feeling pressure to join in on the mistreatment of others, and for help resisting pressure to smoke, curse, and play video games and watch movies that their parents have deemed off-limits. In 1981, Howard wrote, "All my friends are popular. But every time I hang around with them, I get in trouble. How can I be with the friends I like and not get into trouble? If I don't hang around them, I do nothing at recess!"

For every child struggling to keep a friend, there seems to be a child struggling to make a friend.

The mail we receive tells us that the highs and lows of childhood friendship have changed very little. . . .

In 1989, Robert wrote, "There are no boys in my neighborhood . . . every time I invite someone over, I get scared that he will get bored and not like me." A reader named Anne wrote, "I am super shy. It's hard to make friends. I feel that when I try to talk, nothing comes out." For some of these kids, wanting and needing friends is not enough. They need extra encouragement and clear guidance to help them move forward.

In essence, all the letters we receive about friendship reflect every child's wish to have quality relationships, whether the friend is casual or one with whom they have a strong bond—their BFF. We see kids' eagerness to talk about their many friendship dilemmas as evidence that

> We hope our friendship conversations with kids will lead them to think more deeply about what it means to be and have a true friend. . . .

they are tackling the hard work of self-understanding—trying to figure out who they are, what's important to them, and how they want to be treated.

We hope our friendship conversations with kids will lead them to think more deeply about what it means to be and have a true friend—about the value of investing in the deep bonds of friendships versus simply aspiring to be popular. We want them to learn that while disagreements are part and parcel of friendship, problems can be sorted out and conflicts can be resolved. When a friendship has run its course, we hope they feel inclined to show kindness even as they move on—treating others as they would like to be treated. When they ask, "What should I do?" we listen and acknowledge their feelings and suggest ways they can take an active role in managing their relationships. We know that's how kids learn best.

Of course, friendship is not all problem-solving. Kids are also thinking about friendship in optimistic, positive ways. In fact, many of the original poems and drawings kids share with us are celebrations of friendship. Particularly endearing are their charming, guileless drawings of best friends, hands clasped or arms wound around one another, the swoosh of big smiles on their faces. In words and pictures, kids often beautifully illustrate the joy of friendship.

Friends infuse kids' lives with play and companionship, and help them grow as people. Having a circle of friends puts kids in a place where they can work daily on becoming their best selves—friendly, socially competent, empathetic, and confident. People others can count on. People who will make the world a better place, because they're in it.

THE LETTERS

Dear Highlights,
My friend Veronica wants to be my best friend. But I already have one. What shall I do?

—Maria, 1987

Dear Highlights,
I have a lot of friends at school but no best friend. What can I do?

—Sarah, 2002

Dear Sarah,

There is no rule that says that you have to have only one best friend. Each friend is special in a certain way. Perhaps one is a good listener and is always there for you. Other friends may make you laugh or help you with schoolwork. And one might enjoy the same types of movies or books. So, in a way, each friend can be your best friend.

Dear Editor,
I have a problem. There is only one girl on our street my age. She always is on vacation, so when she's not home I have nobody to play with. All the other kids on my street are brats. Can you help me?

—Stacy, age 9, 1976

Dear Highlights,
I have a really bratty friend, or that's what my mom calls her. I agree with my mom, this friend has really good nice times, but when she wants her way, I have to go back to my house. My parents are no help. My friend doesn't let me touch her things, but she touches all over my things. She is the only kid my age in the neighborhood. The other girls are even worse. I really need help!

—Alyssa, 2015

Dear Stacy,

There are many children like you. Often when we think we are not going to like people, we do enjoy them when we know them better. Perhaps there are interesting girls and boys among those you call "brats." Try to get to know them; you may be surprised.

If you can't find children to play with, get books from the library. Any reading you do now will help you later.

We're sure that you will think of many things to do when you really try.

Dear Highlights magazine,

Hi I'm 10 years old.
My friends has a problem with
me. You see everything I like she doesn't
like! She doesn't like the clothes I like
or the music I like, I mean it's like
she doesn't like anything in my whole life.
She even gets in fights with me because
of the people I like or the things.
Can you please help me I going out
of my mind!!!!

—Fatima, 1999

Dear Fatima,

You could try talking privately to your friend about this. Choose a time when you are getting along well with each other. You might say, "I like having you as a friend, but sometimes I become frustrated. You don't seem to like anything or anyone I like. I respect your interests and choices. I understand that a person may like different things and have different friends than I would choose. If everyone liked the same people and things, the world would be very boring. The next time we have a difference of opinion about music or anything else, why don't we just change the subject? We can just decide that we have different ideas about the subject and that neither one of us is going to change our minds." Listen carefully to what your friend has to say.

If your friend still attempts to argue with you, you might say, "I'm going to leave now because we're going to get into a fight about this. That's not good for our friendship. Maybe we'll both be in a better mood another day." Then just leave and go near other friends or go home.

You might also consider spending more time with other people and developing new friendships. It wouldn't mean that you care any less for this friend. Each friend you make has something special to offer you in friendship, and you can never have too many friends.

Dear Highlights,
Everyone at school thinks I am dumb because I play with girls. And I am a boy. Please give me some advice.

—Ryan, 1980

Dear Ryan,

We cannot believe that everyone at school thinks you are dumb because you play with girls. We think you are probably exaggerating. There may be a few people who tease you about being with girls. It's our guess that some boys may tease you because they are not comfortable with girls. As you get older, you will find that boys and girls work together and play together, and no one teases anybody about it. Just try to be yourself and be a friend to all the people you like—whether they are boys or girls.

Dear Highlights,
My classmate and I were best friends last year but now he doesn't show much interest in me. Please help me out.

—Derek, 2001

Dear Derek,

Sometimes people get busy with new activities and don't spend as much time with friends as they once did. That doesn't mean that they don't care anymore. When you have an opportunity, talk to your friend alone. Tell him that you miss spending time with him. Then listen to what he has to say. It is possible that he is upset with you, but he may just be going through a busy time. By talking about the situation, the two of you may find ways to spend more time together.

What is a Friend?

How do you know
if someone is a friend?
For me it's a person
who stands by you till the end.

A person who cares,
someone who shares.

A person who sticks around
when you're feeling down.

A person who's fair,
someone who's always there.

A friend betrays you never,
and a friend lasts forever.
—Mark, age 11, 1997

—Maleah, age 7, 2005

Dear Highlights,
I'm a romance kind of guy, but my friends HATE it. can you help?

—Chase, age 8, 2014

Dear Chase,

There is nothing wrong with being a romantic, and it's nice that you can accept who you are even if your friends haven't yet. We hope you won't try to change yourself for the sake of your friends. True friends will accept you for who you are.

If you haven't already, we encourage you to talk to your friends and ask them why they dislike how romantic you are. Perhaps they feel jealous, or perhaps they feel you talk about romantic things too much and it makes them feel uncomfortable. Whatever the reason, listen carefully and try to understand their point of view. Talking to them may help you figure out how you can be a better friend to them and vice versa.

Dear Highlights,
I am eleven years old. I have a crush on these two cute boys. I really like them! What should I do?

—Shannon, age 11, 1983

Dear Shannon,

The best way to act around boys you like is to be yourself. If you are fun to be with and easy to talk to, boys and girls will like you. Don't worry about boyfriends or crushes yet. Spend time having fun with many friends, both boys and girls. You will enjoy yourself a lot more than if you spend all your time worrying about whether a particular boy likes you or not, and you will probably end up finding that boys like you better that way, too.

Dear Highlights,
I am 10
I need help.

All my friends at school are
saying santa is not real
or they doubt santa but
I still want to beiive
in ~~santa~~ Help!!
santa

—Taylor, age 10, 2015

Dear Taylor,

Our suggestion is to trust what you believe. Every person has a right to his or her beliefs, and it's OK if your beliefs are different from another person's. It's everyone's job to think carefully and make up his or her mind. This will be true all your life. Sometimes you will decide to keep an open mind because you can't really know the answer. Sometimes your beliefs may change as you get older and learn more. But it's still important to make up your own mind and have faith in what you believe.

Whenever we think about those we love and want to give them something special because of our love for them, we show the true spirit of Christmas. When others say that they don't believe in Santa, you might choose to respect their beliefs, but also share with them your feelings in a kind and caring way. For example, you might say something such as, "Thanks for being honest. Right now, I choose to believe in the spirit of giving that Santa brings to Christmas."

You might want to talk to your parents about this. They will have good advice for you.

Dear Highlights,

Some of my friends smoke. So do I, but I don't inhale. They say why smoke, if you don't inhale? So now I've been inhaling. Every time I'm with them I have to smoke. I don't know why I'm doing it. I mean, my parents and brother smoke. I always tell them to stop. What do I do?

—C. M., 1992

Dear C. M.,

We can understand why you feel confused. Sometimes we want to make friends so badly that we forget our priorities. So even though you tell your parents to stop smoking, you're willing to try it to keep some friends.

It might help to think about what you look for in friends. Do you want them to tell you how to act or what to do? And do you think good, true friends would want you to do something harmful to yourself? If your friends won't like you for not smoking, are they really your friends? It sounds as if they think friendship is only about intimidation.

We know it will be difficult, but talk with your family about this. Let them know that you're feeling influenced by others' smoking habits. Talk with them about your fears of losing your friends. They may have experienced similar feelings and may have some good advice for you. They can probably tell you, too, how difficult it is to stop smoking once it becomes a habit.

Dear Highlights,

My friend has her own cell phone. Whenever we play, all she wants to do is use her cell phone with me. I feel like she wants to impress me or something, or she simply has no interest in me. I'm starting to get a little jealous, and I hate feeling jealous. When we were younger, we didn't have cell phones. We'd play non-cell phone games. I wish things were the way they used to be.

—Colleen, 2015

Dear Highlights,

I'm a military kid. Have been all my life. Usually we move to a military base, but my dad just moved to the reserves. So we moved to a small town, where nobody ever moves and everybody knows everybody. To be the odd ball out is hard, and it doesn't help that I'm terrible at making friends. Any suggestions on how to make friends and settle better?

—Anonymous, 2016

Dear Friend,

We believe it is your attitude that will help you the most as you settle in and begin to make friends. People are naturally attracted to those who put forth a cheerful, confident, and positive attitude. While you may be anything but confident, people can't see that. They see your countenance: the look on your face and the way you carry your body.

A person who is shy or who feels uncertain of herself usually slouches, looks downward, and doesn't have many smiles to share with others. She will usually stand back and wait for others to notice and speak to her first. What we encourage you to do is the exact opposite. Stand up tall, smile, and give them a cheerful, "Hi!" Keep moving forward by saying something such as, "My name is _____. I'm new here, so I could sure use some help." If you are quick to offer friendship, others will be encouraged to react in an equally friendly way.

As you begin to meet others, try to focus on them—the things that they are interested in—rather than on your own feelings of insecurity. Show a genuine interest in the things they talk about. You don't have to share their interests in order to show acceptance of them as unique individuals. Participate in activities. Ask if you may sit with a group at lunch.

We don't believe that you are terrible at making friends. We do believe that it's been hard for you to do this over and over again. You can't change that, but you can definitely change your approach to the situation. Friendship is as important to those in your new community as it is to you. Even though those in your class have already built friendships, that doesn't mean there isn't room for someone new. There absolutely is. Try to be patient and positive as you enter each day. We are confident that in a short time, you will be feeling at home in both the community and at school.

Friends

— Brett, age 9, 2014

My friend Jordan and I
are different in a few ways.
He is white and I am brown.
He has brown hair and I have black hair.
He is shorter and I am taller,
but who cares?
That's what friends are all about.

     —Carlos, age 8, 2008

Dear Highlights,

I've known my best friend for three years. Her and I are closer than sisters. She has two disorders though. Her disorders cause her to act annoying, obnoxious, etc. She doesn't do this on purpose. The disorders make her act like that without warning, and people judge her because of this. She's having a really hard time dealing with this because her "friends" will get mad at her when her disorders make her act differently, but they don't know about her disorders. It hurts me to see her in so much despair. I need to help her. Please help.

—Jasmine, 2012

Dear Jasmine,

One thing you might do is encourage your friend to have one-on-one conversations with her other close friends, and let them know that she appreciates them, even when she has trouble controlling her behavior. There is no need for your friend to share information about her disorders, unless she feels comfortable doing so. Just by acknowledging the fact that she acts differently sometimes and assuring her friends that she doesn't mean to hurt their feelings, she may improve her friendships. You can also urge your friend to talk with her parents and her doctor about her friendship concerns. Her doctor may be able to suggest techniques for managing her outbursts and avoiding uncomfortable social situations. Your school counselor might also be able to support your friend.

Ultimately, you can't control your friend's actions, or prevent others from judging her, as much as you might want to. You can, however, tell her that you'll always care about her and be willing to listen when she's upset. One patient listener can make a world of difference to someone who's unhappy.

Dear Highlights,
Nobody likes this girl in my class but me. If hang out with her, nobody will like me. What should I do?

—Allison, 1989

Dear Allison,

A friend is someone you enjoy being with, a person you can trust and have fun with. If you enjoy being with the girl, she may make a good friend. You might think about how you would feel if no one liked you. It must be very difficult for this girl to come to school each day knowing that she has no one to spend time with. You are the only one who can decide who your friends will be. Don't let the other kids in your class decide for you. If you decide that you would rather not be close friends with this girl, you can still be nice to her. If others see you being kind to her, they may act in the same way.

Dear Highlights,
My friend has some other friends who are a little mean. I'm starting to be left out. They're teaming up on me in games. What should I do?

—Jeff, 2000

Dear Jeff,

Long-lasting friendships are developed over a period of time with a lot of effort. As we grow, our interests don't always match those of our friends. And often, new friendships have an impact on existing ones. Sometimes when new people enter the picture, others are so intrigued by them that they chase after them to make friends, not realizing that their present friends might be hurt. It may take your friend awhile to realize that being mean to win the friendship of others is wrong and unkind. Don't be unkind to your friend. Smile when you see him, but don't join his games. Look for others in your neighborhood or classroom who enjoy doing things you like and who will be more respectful. If you do your best to understand, then your friendship may heal in time. If it does not improve, then you will have begun to make other friends who will treat you more kindly.

Dear Highlights,

My friends and I are going through the stage in our young teen years when we want to have a boyfriend, just to show off. of my good friends doesn't have a boyfriend so some girls were trying to hook her up. About a day after this she took me aside at recess and said, "Tell them that I don't want a boyfriend or something!"

"Why? You're great looking! You know that you can have a guy if you wanted!" I replied.

"No," she stated. "It's not like that! Don't tell anyone this, but I don't want a guy. I want a girl friend." She said giving me a puppy dog look that says, "It's not my fault!"

I couldn't believe my ears! "YOUR GAY?" I shouted, forgetting myself.

Just then a group of girls happened to be walking by, chitter-chattering away. When they heard this, they stopped dead in their tracks, staring, mouths open wide, before turning around.

My friend stared at me with wide eyes and then marched away. And (surprise, surprise) one hour later every one in the world knew that my friend was … gay. They made fun of her and denied ever being her friend.

I feel very bad and mixed up. Can you please help? I try to be her friend, but every time that I look at her I get a horrible feeling. How can I keep being her friend? Hurt and lost.

—Alexandra, age 12, 2003

Dear Alexandra,

We can understand how bad you must feel to have caused your friend's embarrassment. All of us have done things that we wish we could undo. But life isn't like that. The best we can do is try to make amends for what we have done and learn from the experience. Experiences can help us grow stronger and wiser.

We're glad you want to be this girl's friend. If she is being teased by the others in your class, it sounds as if a friend is what she needs most right now. Our readers tell us how much it helps to have just one person stand up for them when others are teasing them.

You said that what's making it hard for you to be her friend is that you get a horrible feeling when you look at her. We couldn't tell if you mean you feel bad because she's gay or because you embarrassed her. If it's because she's gay, we'd like to suggest some things that may help: Your friend is no different than she was before she told you she was gay. The things you liked about her and that made you friends then are still true. Also, each person has the right to be an individual. Our differences enrich us and make life more interesting. Your friend has the right to be different and to be respected.

If what is bothering you is that you're feeling guilty or sad about what happened, then we suggest you talk to your friend and let her know how you feel. Let her know that you are sorry for what happened. Listen carefully to what she has to say, too. By talking honestly and calmly about what happened, you might be able to get your friendship back on track.

You might also consider talking to the girls who are teasing her. Without getting angry or accusing anyone, you could explain why you think their behavior is unfair. Your honesty and thoughtfulness may make them think again about what they are doing.

You may want to talk to your mom or dad or another adult you trust about this problem. A relative, teacher, school counselor, or clergyperson are good people to talk to. People who care about you would want to know if you are upset about something, and they may have good suggestions for you.

Dear Highlights,
I have austism (high functioning) I am a social butterfly but when it comes to keeping freinds I have a problem to that. Social skills is a problem for me. Do you have any tips???

—Maya, age 11, 2013

Dear Maya,

In our experience, we've found one of the best ways to keep friends is to treat them the way you would want to be treated. Listen to them when they talk, be considerate of the things they like, and always be kind to them. If a person feels comfortable with you and shares similar interests, they will likely want to be your friend.

We can understand that these things may be difficult for you because of your autistic tendencies. This is why we think it's important for you to reach out to adults who know you well, ideally adults who are familiar with autism. You can learn to keep friends—it just may take some time. We hope you will be patient with yourself. Everyone has something that he or she struggles with. Often, with the right support, we can all find ways to succeed.

—Robert, age 8, 1993

Gray

Gray is a lonely heart
waiting for someone to come along.
    Gray is like a cold rainy day in the fall
bringing sadness and a broken heart together.
    Gray is lazy, when you can't move
in the morning.
    Gray is when it's black outside
and not a big orange sun.
    Gray is when your bright yellow balloon
flies away.
    Gray is when your best friend
moves away.

—Sarah, age 11, 1994

Dear Highlights,
My friend and I have been fighting a lot lately. We're content at school, but when we get on social media at night or on the weekends, we always fight! I don't want to fight, but then she hits me where it hurts with being against one of my beliefs, and I become infuriated. Usually she starts going on about me being a horrible friend and that she is better friends with people who, frankly, talk behind her back about her flaws! I know what you're thinking, "You shouldn't hold on to a friend like this!" But here's the problem, there's only 4 girls in my class: one of them has things with me in common (my "BFF"), there's one that constantly verbally stabs me in the back (she says bad things behind my back), and the other one talks bad about my friend. Without my BFF, I literally have NO female friends at my school. Feel me here, ok?

                                                        —Anonymous, 2016

Dear Friend,

We're sorry to hear that you and your friend have been fighting on social media. As you've discovered, communication over the internet can often lead to conflict. Sometimes it's because we feel as though we are less accountable for our words and actions when we are hidden behind our computer screens, rather than being face-to-face. Sometimes social media makes it easier for us not to be our best selves, letting more immature, petty, and unkind actions and words come through. We find that the best way to avoid conflict on social media is to limit social-media use. Make an active, conscious choice to stop all online communication with friends you fight with online. Decide for yourself that any conversations—whether serious or not—need to happen in person with this friend. You might even start by letting her know, face-to-face, that you are going to be limiting your social-media time in order to avoid conflict. Then, follow through!

  If your friend starts a conversation with you online, you might simply say, "I'm sorry, I can't talk through this social-media site right now. Let's catch up about this tomorrow." Then, sign off. This strategy will also give your friend time to calm down and cool off before talking to you the next day. And if you are together and a sensitive topic that often leads to fighting comes up, you might simply excuse yourself or change the subject. Refuse to get drawn into arguments over difficult topics. Instead, keep the focus on the things you have in common. This is the best way to support a healthy, happy friendship.

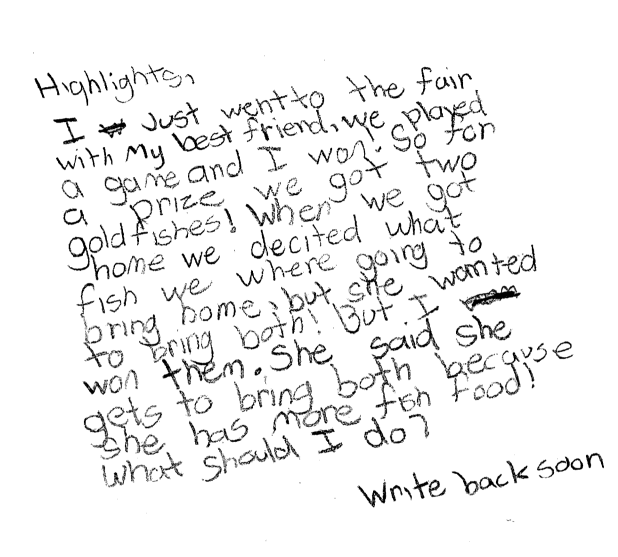

Highlights,

I ~~≠~~ Just went to the fair
with my best friend, we played
a game and I won. So for
a prize we got two
goldfishes! When we got
home we decited what
fish we where going to
bring home, but she wanted
to bring both. But I wanted
won them. She said she
gets to bring both because
she has more fish food!
What should I do?

Write back soon

—Ashlyn, age 10, 2013

Dear Ashlyn,

This sounds like an uncomfortable situation. Sharing is always a nice thing to do, but if your parents have given you permission to keep one of the goldfish, then you don't have to give your friend both goldfish. Try calmly talking with your friend about why you want to keep a goldfish. Assure her that you will be able to get your own fish food and properly care for your fish.

If she insists on taking both goldfish home, you can certainly tell your friend, "I know you like the goldfish, but I like them, too, and I want to keep one of them." Then, in an effort to change her focus, you can say, "Let's talk about something else," or "Let's get back to having fun."

Your mom and dad might have some other good suggestions for you.

Dear Highlights,
I have had a friend since first grade. Now in fourth grade, she is very different from first grade. I want to tell her I don't want to hang out with her anymore, but I can't get her to understand. Please help me!

—David, 2000

Dear David,

Everyone changes over time, but it can be hard to see a friend change so much that you no longer want to be around her. Perhaps this friend is not aware of what she is doing or saying that bothers you. Talking with her about it may give you a chance to save the friendship.

If you do discuss this with her, try to speak calmly and politely. Tell her your feelings, and don't blame her. Also give her a chance to express her thoughts and be sure to listen carefully. Listening is one of the best ways to understand how someone else is feeling. After you've done these things, you may still want to end the friendship. If you decide to do this, tell her kindly but firmly.

Dear Higlights,

There is a girl in another class at my school who I used to be friends with. A few weeks ago, she said I ruined her life. I know what she is talking about, and she tried to say sorry, but I just wasn't ready to forgive her. I have a feeling she'll try to say sorry again. If she does, what should I do?

Me

Her

—Annabelle, 2017

Dear Annabelle,

You're not alone. We often hear from kids who have had a disagreement with a friend.

It might help if the two of you could talk for a few minutes when there aren't a lot of other people around. Calmly tell your friend that you value the friendship and want to figure out ways to get along better. Listen to what she has to say. By talking about the problems, the two of you may find a solution.

It can be frustrating when people do things that bother you, but we can see that you already understand that getting angry will not make the situation better. When someone makes you angry, try to step back from the situation for a moment. If possible, instead of responding to what is said or done that makes you angry, calmly walk away from the person who upset you. Then you might find that it is easier to respond in a calmer way or to ignore what has been said or done—and a disagreement might be avoided. It's also important for you to treat your friend with kindness and respect, as you would like to be treated. If there are things that you do that bother her, try to stop doing those things. Eventually, you may see that she is treating you more nicely, too.

All alone
New again
Another day
Full of pain
But you turn
And see someone
Who asks,
"Will you be my friend?"

—Asad, age 11, 2003

—Stephanie, age 5, 1951

Letters About

Feelings

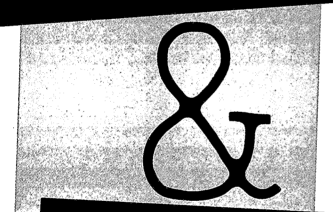

&

Confidence

A BIG PART OF CHILDHOOD IS LEARNING HOW to manage feelings. Over the decades, tens of thousands of children have written to *Highlights* for help with identifying, understanding, and expressing their thoughts and emotions. Many children reach out because they have been denied the chance to express themselves at home. Others write to us because they are afraid that if they share their feelings, they might be dismissed, shamed, misunderstood, or cause others pain or disappointment.

Feelings! They can be complicated and hard to unpack. They can confuse and overwhelm kids—and even frighten them. In this chapter, we share letters and emails from kids who are having trouble identifying and understanding their own strong emotions, like Jay, who in 1997 wrote: "I have a problem that I need help solveing. I worry about such little things that I don't have to worry about. Please give me advice because I need it fast." Julia, a *Highlights* reader in 2004, wrote that she is grumpy every night and just wants everyone to stay away from her. "I lock myself in my room. I've considered running away or anything to get away from this world." Is it hormones, she wondered?

We still see many letters from children who are struggling with feelings of shame, humiliation, or rejection after being scorned or ridiculed. Teasing, it seems, is as old as childhood, and generations of readers have told us that they've either experienced teasing or live in fear that they will encounter it. Kids tell us they are teased about their looks, their abilities, their preferences, their ethnicity, their religion, and more. For some children, the teasing cuts deep.

Conflict at home is another common theme we see, and it can leave kids with a tangle of emotions.

Other kids seek our help because they worry about adult problems. In 1982, Tracy wrote: "I always hear my mom and dad talking about how taxes have gone up and money is really tight. What I want to know is to either ask for less stuff at Christmas or just ask for regular stuff so they wouldn't know that I know about our money, and should I worry?"

Conflict at home is another common theme we see, and it can leave kids with a tangle of emotions. In 2006, James wrote about both his fear and anger when his parents fought: "I love my parents but I HATE it when my dad yells and screams at my mom. It makes me scared and sometimes I want to hit him to make him stop. What should I do?"

And, just like adults, kids can experience feelings of loneliness and fear that they may be misfits. "Do my parents love me?" one nameless reader wrote in an email in 2000. "They said no and say go away! But sometimes they say they love me and would do anything for me. Do they mean it?" A few years later, Kimberly wrote this: "I need to know how I can feel welcome and not alone. I feel like I don't have many friends and like theirs nothing in this world for me. I feel so stressed over life. Do you have any advice to help me enjoy life?" In 2004, David had a similar concern but put it this way: "Dear Highlights, I hope you can help me. I don't feel like myself, and I've been lost for almost a year."

As adults with the benefit of hindsight, we might be tempted to minimize the pain of childhood, especially if we came out OK on the other side. Or, if we remember our own childhood pain, we might overly protect children. And, for some of us, our memory of childhood is spotty, and we've simply forgotten how deeply affected we were as children by problems that may seem inconsequential to us now. We might even wonder if it's possible to pay too much attention to children's questions and concerns, raising a generation that thinks the world is all about them. But the numbers of letters we receive with more extrème expressions of stress and worry have increased in recent years. Kids write to us more often about cutting, eating disorders, and mental illness. It's always been true, but it's especially true today: Children need practice expressing their thoughts and feelings. They need a safe space where they can explore their feelings with empathetic adults who listen

It's always been true, but it's especially true today: Children need practice expressing their thoughts and feelings.

and validate all their feelings, even the uncomfortable ones.

In our responses to these kinds of letters, we strive to offer a lot of compassion and little judgment. We listen carefully to help clarify what's confusing to the child and to gently point out any interpretations that may be false or inaccurate. We assure them that what they are feeling is normal, which often lifts the burden of shame (a particularly confusing and debilitating emotion) some children carry. We also reassure them that "this too shall pass"—that their feelings won't swallow them up or last forever. Feelings can change, especially as we learn and apply calming and coping skills. Learning some steps they can take to make

By taking seriously the thoughts of children ... we are telling them they matter and that what they think matters.

things better can give them a sense of control and agency. When we deliver this kind of nurturing support, we teach kids both when and how to ask for help, and we empower them to learn how to work through their emotions.

Most importantly, by taking seriously the thoughts of children who are confused, worried, embarrassed, or frightened, we are sending kids the powerful message that they are worthy of our time and our concern. We are telling them that they matter and that what they think matters. We never know with certainty whether we are serving as a touchstone for a young person navigating the normal ups and downs of childhood—or whether we are a lifeline, particularly these days when anxiety in children is increasingly common and serious. We only know that both roles matter deeply.

THE LETTERS

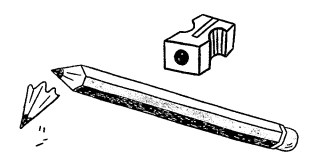

Dear Highlights,
Every once in a while, I get a chain mail that scares me a lot. It's often about really tragic stuff that will happen if I don't post the e-mail. The images get stuck in my head. I'm too scared to look on websites to see if they are true or not. HELP PLEASE!
—Anonymous, 2010

Dear Highlights,
Sometimes I watch YouTube videos and see creepy stuff. Sometimes I get so scared I can't sleep or have a stomachache. What do I do?
—Ariana, 2019

Dear Ariana,

We're sorry to hear that sometimes you get curious and click on YouTube videos that make you feel scared and upset. We know the temptation to satisfy your curiosity is a hard one to resist, but we're proud of you for noticing this pattern and wanting to change it. This is the first and most important step toward making things better.

In order to resist your curiosity to click on creepy-looking videos, we encourage you to talk to your parents about putting limits on your YouTube account. Ask your parents to look into blocking or limiting the creepy videos available to you on YouTube. They might also remove the "suggested videos" feature so that one creepy video won't lead to many more. You might also talk with your parents about making a deal that you will watch YouTube only in shared family spaces, where others can see and hear what you are watching. When you're supervised, we hope it will be easier to resist this curiosity. And with time and practice, you will be a better judge of what is good to watch.

Dear Highlights,

I once wrote to you before w/ a piece of art. Now I come for advice. My dad is in the military and he's away for six months. We can't know where, and It's really hard. I act up and can calm myself. Please help! What should I do when I'm mad? I'm nervous and driving my mom nuts. Please write back! I'm 9 years old and should control myself. Help!

— Nervous in New Jersey

P. S. I'd like to be called that, Thanks!

—Clara, age 9, 2017

Dear Clara,

In our experience, it's hard to stop feelings from occurring. But while we can't always control how we feel, we can control how we act. The next time you feel your anger building, you could say, "I am starting to feel upset, so I need to take a break," then quietly find a place to be alone. Take deep breaths as you count to ten.

Another idea is to channel your feelings into a positive activity, such as drawing, writing, or exercising. You might even decide to write in a journal. You could also use your journal to keep track of your daily activities so you can tell your dad all about them when you get the chance. Or you could draw pictures and write stories to give to your dad when he returns.

We also encourage you to talk to your mom about this. You can also talk to another trusted adult. Sometimes upset feelings are like boiling water in a covered pot—they bubble and bubble, and get hotter and hotter, until they can't be contained anymore. Sharing a concern is like lifting the cover off the pot—heat is released and the bubbling becomes much less, or it stops entirely.

We're glad you wrote to us, and we hope this helps. Your dad is doing a brave thing for our country, and we appreciate his dedication and service.

Dear Monica,

We're sorry that Father's Day brings up sad memories for you. We can understand that it is difficult for you to have a holiday dedicated to fathers. For us, we like to think that Father's Day is celebrating more than just biological fathers. We extend it to any kind of father figure, or even to future fathers. This can include grandpas, uncles, brothers, cousins, family friends, stepdads, foster dads, and more.

You will meet many people in your life who care about you and want to help you succeed. They will offer you advice, comfort, and support. They will help you feel loved. Instead of thinking about your father who left when you were two, think about all of the men who have stayed in your life in some way or another. Be grateful to them and what they have done for you. We're sure they will appreciate the gesture.

If you haven't spoken to your mom yet about how you feel, we hope you will. She loves you very much, and she wants you to be happy. We're sure if she knew this was bothering you, she would want to help you feel better. She may have some more advice for you as well.

Dear Highlights,

I am nine years old. My dad left when I was 2 and he came back. I am sad that Fathers day is coming up and don't want to celebrate. Everybody wants me to but it makes me sad. What do I do

—Monica, age 9, 2015

Behind the Mask

Behind the Mask
There is a girl
Smart as a peacock
Bright as a pearl

But she doesn't want to grow up
It's sad but true
If you're like her
You're afraid to be you

Behind the Mask
A girl does lie
Small and scared
Timid and shy

—Hannah, age 11, 2004

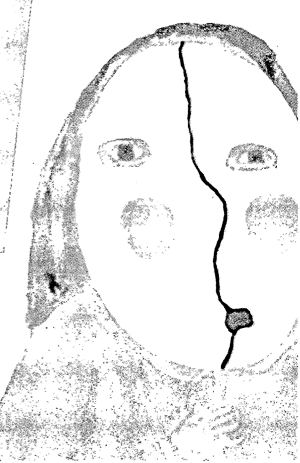

—David, age 11, 2013

Afraid

When you are afraid
Your body shakes,
Your heart pounds faster.
Sometimes you cry.
You want to hide.
You want to run away.
You go to your mom so she
Can hug you, and tell you
Everything will be Ok.

—Josh, age 9, 1992

I was bullied for the last 2 school years witch has changed my atitude from nice to mean. So now my temper is bad, I don't know how to let my temper out without being mean and hurting other people including my friends. What should I do?

—Dakota, 2014

Dear Dakota,

We're so sorry to hear that you have been bullied. That is a hard thing to experience. We can understand why it has affected your behavior, but we hope you won't accept that this is the way you have to be forever.

How we feel is a choice, Dakota. You can either choose to be happy about life or you can be upset. If you choose to be happy, you may find that the things that caused you to get angry before don't seem so important anymore.

Likewise, how we act is also a choice. If you lash out at your friends and family when you are angry, you are behaving no differently than the bullies that caused you to feel so bad for two years. The people closest to you are the people you should be treating with the most kindness and respect.

Dear Highlights,

I have this problem about fear. I am in fourth grade. When my mom gets home she's to tired to listen. My sister never wants to listen. Well I do not no if you can save my problem but I had to tell someone.

Well my fear is about crimes and disasters. At night I lie in bed and think about things that can happen to me. I think about fires and earthquakes. Then I hear sounds and I think about crimes. There are a lot of crimes. I try not to think about it but I do. I still keep trying. I hope you can help.

–Danielle, 1983

Dear Danielle,

The news we hear is frightening. However, if we think about these things all of the time, we can feel very low and depressed. There really is not too much that we can do to change big problems like this. Our government leaders and state officials are elected by us to handle these major problems. We have to have faith and trust in them and hope that they will do a good job.

We think it is extremely important for you to share your thoughts with your mother. We understand that she is busy and that she works. But we are sure that Mom would set aside some time to sit and talk with you about your thoughts. We are also sure that you would feel better. The main thing is not to keep it inside so that it hurts you.

When you are going to bed at night, you might try a relaxation exercise. Close your eyes and think about a special place where you would like to be. Maybe it's Disney World or a tropical island. Imagine yourself there and let the good feelings come over you. After you have settled yourself into this "fantasy," you might find it a lot easier to calm down and fall asleep. Another way to prepare for bedtime and relaxation is to read a fun book. Reading is a great way to relax! It's important to slow an active mind down so it can rest and regroup for the next day.

Dear Highlights,

I've always had trouble with my self esteem and looks although people frequently say I'm pretty and smart. Though inside, I feel rotten to the core. I feels as if I don't deserve the life I am living. I have a wonderful, loving family, a very nice house to live in, and almost everything I could ever want. Although my mom always says I'm very special, I don't feel like it at all. Actually, I kind of just feel like a puppet. Meaning, I never form own opinions and just repeat what others say. I know inside that I'm not as smart or clever as other people claim. Please give me tips on dealing with these feelings.

—Caitlin, age 14, 2013

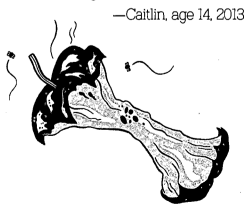

Dear Caitlin,

We can tell from your letter that you ARE indeed a smart and very special girl. As for imitating what other people say, we think a certain amount of that is natural while you're young and "trying out" different opinions and ways of expressing yourself. It's a sign of maturity that you're contemplating any of this at all (that you're seeking your individuality).

If you don't already write in a journal, we suggest trying it out. It's a great place to work out some things that are worrying you and to practice articulating your thoughts and opinions about things. You could also make a list of things you like about yourself, as well as good things happening in your life. We know it's hard to let yourself believe that you're pretty or smart when you don't feel that way inside, but we recommend trying to accept it. As you grow in confidence, we think accepting this will become easier.

When you're getting too stuck "in your head," it's good to mix it up and do other things you enjoy. Focusing on positive things will probably help you feel better.

We wish you a wonderful year of being 14!

Dear highlights,

I just found out that I'm moving away from memories, from friends, from school and from and I have to move to a new school. Which is terri-fi-ing. Beause I'm going to junior high! AAAAhhhh! Plus I have to move in to an apartment and I just moved from a big two storie house. How am i supposed to cop with that! I'm moving from Boise Idaho to Mountin home, Idaho. I'm in a pickle and I'm scared. Highlights can you tell me how to fuel better and not totally freak my socks off! There are so many butterflies in my tummy and i'm so stressed. Help me!

I'M trapped!!

High Idaho

Moving truck

School
Apartment
Moving
Highlights

—Deedee, age 12, 2013

Dear Deedee,

It might help to work on a project preserving your memories of your house. You can start a "House Memories Scrapbook" and put the photos in the scrapbook, along with other photos of fun times you've had in your house. Walk through every room and make a list of things you remember about that room—funny stories, good memories, things you'll miss. Then you can put the list under each photo.

We'd encourage you to think of moving as an adventure. You might look into joining some clubs or after-school activities to meet kids who share your interests. If you give yourself time, have a good sense of humor, and let people get to know you, you may make some great friends.

Dear Highlights,
I like to sing and dance, but I get embarassed when someone is watching. Help!
—Brody, age 8, 2014

Dear Brody,

Many people feel embarrassed when they know that others are watching them sing and dance. Just knowing that others experience the same thing might help you feel better!

If you would like to overcome this, you might want to practice singing and dancing in front of family members. When you feel comfortable with that, you can share your talent with friends. The more you practice in front of others, the more comfortable you can become.

You might want to ask your teacher for some suggestions. For example, when some people perform on stage, they look over the top of the audience members' heads to the back of the room. They are more comfortable because they are not looking into the eyes of the audience members.

If you continue to feel embarrassed, that's OK. You need to accept yourself for who you are. Remind yourself of the strengths you have. Even if you are a great singer and dancer, you may need to develop some more confidence in your ability until you can perform in front of others. Be patient and stick with the singing and dancing if you enjoy it. Eventually, we believe you'll be ready to share your talent with others. It can bring joy to many people!

Dear Highlights,

These are some things I live by:

· Speak only when spoken to (This rule only applies with my parents pretty much)

· No one cares how you feel, so put a smile on your face and pretend you're fine

· Do what others want you to do, not what you want to do*

· Tell only good lies and some truth**

· Cry at night when people think you're asleep

· Know that whatever you do, you're going to fail***

· Never ask for anything

· When people ask you if you want anything, always say 'no'

* Well, not like do drugs or alcohol. But if someone tells you to jump off a cliff and you don't want to, you still need to jump off a cliff

** Good lies are lies that make others happy, even if it's not what you want to say. (Example: My mom asks every day, "How was your day?" Every day I reply quickly, "Good. (Lie)" Then quickly change the subject and ask how her day was. She probably doesn't really want to know how my day was, she's just trying to be polite. Plus, she doesn't deserve to have my burdens on her shoulders along with her own)

***This one only applies to me personally. No one else in this world fails as much as I do.

Here's the problem. I break my own code all the time. Today I talked to my mom a few times without her talking to me first. How can I keep my code? It seems so hard!

—Kyla, 2015

Dear Kyla,

Maybe this code seems like the easiest way to avoid complication, but you and we know it's not the code you want to live by. We're so sorry you feel as if no one really cares and that you have to pretend things are OK when they're not. It's important to be true to yourself, and pretending won't allow you to do that.

Even though it may seem as if your mom is just asking questions to be polite, we assure you she loves you and wants to know what's on your mind. Sometimes people get busy or have their own problems to deal with and they don't express their affection, but we hope you'll talk with your mom honestly about the way you're feeling. You might even start the conversation by showing her this code. The next time you feel lonely, open up to your parents rather than shying away.

We think it would be a good idea to talk to a guidance counselor at school, too. Many kids go through phases when they consider themselves failures at everything, and we'd bet your guidance counselor has some advice that would help you.

When you're down, it's important to keep doing the activities that make you feel good—making art, music, reading, or spending time outside. You could make cards for people just to let them know you care or try to get to know a shy kid at school. Also, write a list of things you like about yourself, as well as things you're thankful for, then keep this list in a handy place and try adding a new item every day. We can already suggest two items for your list: You are highly intelligent and you're a strong writer. (Our guess is that you also have a great sense of humor—you may just need to use it more!)

—Evan, age 8, 1993

Today

Today I looked at the world in a different way.
I curled up my past and threw it away.
Today I learned something new and different.
I learned to make every day a good day
And not to shut off the world when you're sad, mad,
Or depressed.
So tomorrow, curl up your past and throw it away.

—Emily, age 9, 2002

Dear Highlights,

I'm inside the 5th grade and I already have the beginning of acne. My mom and dad always tell me that "Everyone will go through it. No need to be embarrassed." Well, there's nobody in this class with the same problem. They may have a pimple or two, but I have a total breakout on my forehead. Other kids call me "Zit-Face" and "Acne-Boy." Well I'm tired of it! Not to mention, I've been hiding from my best friend because I'm afraid that she'll think "Eew! Acne! I'm leaving you, Pimple-Man!" I need some help! Please reply ASAP. I'm not sure how long this will go on! It might even effect my place in the popularity chart!

—Anonymous, 2010

Dear Friend,

We're sorry you're worried about acne, and we certainly understand how frustrating it can be. Many of the editors at Highlights remember dealing with pimples at a young age. Even if nobody in your class has skin trouble, we're certain that plenty of our readers share your situation.

We can offer some tips for reducing your breakouts, but we hope you'll also ask your family doctor for advice.

We're always sad to hear about kids teasing other kids. Kids usually tease for two reasons: to get attention and to feel better about themselves. When kids tease you about your pimples, you might pretend not to hear them, or you could simply walk away.

One thing we've found about true friendships is they're always worn "inside-out." That is, they're based on inner qualities, such as kindness, trust, and honesty, rather than on outer appearances. Popularity, on the other hand, is frequently "outside-in"—it often focuses on a person's looks, clothing, toys, or other visible things. Popularity may come and go, since these outer qualities are always changing. True friendship lasts much longer. We believe your best friend appreciates you for many reasons, and we hope you won't let your skin get in the way of your friendship.

Dear Highlights,

The girls at school don't always like me and they say I have the cooties.

You have the cooties. You have the cooties.

It makes me feel like I have the cooties. Please do help.

—Jacob, 2019

Dear Jacob,

You may be relieved to know that you don't have cooties. We know this because no one has cooties—cooties are something that boys and girls made up a very long time ago. You might ask your parents if they heard about cooties when they were your age. They may have helpful ideas for how to react when the girls say you have cooties. Your parents want to know when someone says something that upsets you.

Kids sometimes say things like, "You have cooties!" because they think it is a funny joke. They may not realize how much their words can hurt your feelings. The next time someone says that you have cooties, you might say, "It hurts my feelings when you say that. Please stop." They may stop after they realize that you are upset. If they continue saying it, we encourage you to walk away from them. You might find other friends to play with.

If the girls keep saying things that upset you after you've asked them to stop or walked away, it may be a good idea to let your teacher know. Your teacher's job is to make sure that everyone is happy and comfortable at school.

Remember to spend time doing your favorite activities. You may find that the more time you spend having fun, the less you worry about teasing.

Dear Highlights,

I don't know what to do with my life. I feel empty sometimes. For 11 years of my life, I've been doing what I was told to do. I go to school. I do my homework. I go home, finding the weekend boring. And it continues, like a cycle. I know that I'll grow up. I'll go to high school and college. Then I'd get a job. Then what? Money isn't important to me that much. All I would need is a house for my mom, dad, and myself to live in and food for all of us. Is that it? I feel like I'm not destined to do anything. I don't want to give up my life studying chemicals like a scientist. I don't want to be a mail carrier or anything. I don't want to think about jobs right now. Besides jobs, how can I be happy for my life? I hardly enjoy things now.

—Anonymous, 2010

Dear Friend,

One thing that may help is sharing your feelings with the people who love you. Even if they can't solve your concerns, they can offer comfort by listening.

Another idea is to set daily goals, rather than focusing only on the "big picture." Gaining an education and starting a career are important steps in life, but your day-to-day activities are also meaningful. Maybe you'd like to learn a new hobby or skill, such as playing a musical instrument, speaking a foreign language, creating a collection of stories or art, or participating in a sport. Each day, you could aim to spend time practicing your hobby. When you meet your daily goal, reward yourself with a favorite treat.

Offering kindness or help to others can be a good pick-me-up. You might challenge yourself to engage in one "random act of kindness" each day. Your action could be as simple as smiling at a classmate in the hallway, or paying a compliment to a friend. Even the smallest kind gesture can have a huge, positive effect.

Dear Highlights,

I have a bit of a problem. I love reading books, especially the Harry Potter series. I'm getting through them pretty quickly. My friend and I love talking about getting into Hogwarts (the school of witchcraft and wizardry). My brother, sister, and mom loved reading the books. My dad just watched the movies. And well, my brother and sister didn't get into Hogwarts. And now, that's really all I want. One night I talked about it to my mom when we were watching TV. She said, "It's just a fun thing to read about. Fantasy is something you can enjoy, whether it's real or not." This kinda disappointed me. Being a wizard means everything to me. On my 11th birthday, I don't know what I am gonna do if I don't get a letter!

Please help.

—Alexa, age 10, 2014

Dear Alexa,

We encourage you to have a talk with your parents during a quiet, private time. Express how you are feeling about Harry Potter and your upcoming birthday, and then ask for their advice.

Here are a few other thoughts to keep in mind: There is much more to being a wizard or witch than attending Hogwarts. Harry is a great wizard because he is kind and loyal to his friends, brave and strong against those who are unkind and intend evil, and smart and hardworking. These are traits that will take you far in any school. Many "muggle" schools need kind, respectful students to make their classrooms better places to learn. There are many opportunities to bring magic into your school. For someone who is lonely, upset, or sad, a smile from a classmate or a friendly word of encouragement can have a magical effect.

Instead of focusing on that Hogwarts letter, we suggest that you and your friend use the magic you already have to make the world around you a better place. This is the best magic there is!

Always Near

Happiness, the ultimate goal,
is always there inside,
even during the toughest times,
when you're done and want to hide.

Sometimes, you feel hope is gone,
want to disappear.
Feeling good is within reach.
Good vibes–always near.

Thoughts rule us, happy and sad,
they often control your mind.
Within you there are positive thoughts,
something you can find.

Dig deep, find yourself,
search within your heart.
Happiness is never far
right from the very start.

—Jordan, age 10, 2019

—Heidi, age 7, 2003

Dear Highlights,
I always blame stuff on myself. I also always put myself down and say I'm ugly. I'm really skinny, so everyone picks on me. I blame myself for being skinny, ugly, and stupid. Please help.

—Lucy, 1992

Dear Highlights,
I really need your help! I've been having problems on how I see my body size. I used to be skinny, but lately, my mom and others have been saying how I've grown some meat on my bones. In particular, my legs and cheeks. I want to talk to my parents, but I'm scared, because, over the years, I've grown trust issues for everyone around me. I'm stuck in a cage, and I can't escape!

—Anonymous, 2017

Dear Friend,

We're glad you decided to confide in us. We realize it can be difficult to reach out for help when you feel as though you have trust issues. We often hear from kids who worry about their appearance. You are definitely not alone.

You might mention that the comments about your appearance have been bothering you, and you're having some difficulties about how you see your body size. Sometimes people don't realize how their comments affect others, and once you let them know how you feel, they are less likely to say those things. Perhaps you can ask a parent if they can make an appointment for you to talk to your doctor about your weight and overall health. Your doctor is the best person to let you know whether your weight is healthy for your age and body type. They can also offer tips on eating nutritious meals, getting proper exercise, having a positive body image, and reducing stress.

Even though you're scared to talk to your parents, we hope you will seriously consider talking to them.

You might consider talking with another trusted adult, too, such as an aunt, a grandparent, a favorite teacher, a school counselor, or the school nurse. The important thing to realize is that this isn't something you need to figure out on your own. There are caring people to help you work through it.

Dear Highlights,
I have a problem about controlling my temper at my house. When I'm mad and I'm not at home, I don't do anything. But when I am home, I just go to my room and throw things around. I need your help.

—Luke, 1998

Dear Luke,
You have already taken the first step. When you realized that you have a temper, you developed an awareness, and that is your first step in controlling it. If you feel you are likely to lose your temper, take a few deep breaths, and slowly count to ten until you feel your anger go away. You might realize that losing your temper doesn't really solve anything. You might also try to pretend that you are the other person, and try to imagine what you would feel. As you become more aware of others' feelings, you may get less angry. Once you see the benefits of controlling your temper, you may find that you have the strength to handle stressful situations.

One thing that may help is sharing your feelings with the people who love you. Your mom and dad care very much about your happiness, and they'd want to support you anytime you're anxious or uncertain. Even if they can't solve your concerns, they can offer comfort by listening. You might also choose to talk with a favorite teacher, close friend, or school counselor.

> Dear Highlights,
>
> I'm adopted from Viet Nam. Whenever I sing the National Anthem, I feel like a traitor. WHAT SHOULD I DO ??
>
> —Kerry, 2016

Dear Kerry,

We understand that you feel a sense of loyalty to Vietnam. It's only natural that you would feel this way. We truly believe that the people in your homeland would not think of you as a traitor for singing the U.S. national anthem. In the same way, we believe that people in the U.S. would not think of you as a traitor for singing the Vietnamese national anthem if you get a chance to visit your homeland someday.

Being from Vietnam is a part of who you are, Kerry, and that will never change. You can learn about the people, traditions, and history of your country to make you feel even more connected to your homeland. At the same time, we hope you will also cherish being an American citizen and learning as much as you can about the people, traditions, and history of the U.S. You can honor and love both countries and be proud of it!

Together, you and your parents can learn more about your homeland. If your family doesn't already, you might include some Vietnamese traditions in your home. Together, you can celebrate all that has made you who you are and make plans for the person you grow up to be.

Dear Highlights,

I am eleven years old and have a very big problem. Every time I say something, or do something, I either get yelled at or get interrupted. My mother always tells me to let my feelings out, but when I do, I get yelled at. I tried talking to them about it, but I get yelled at. What should I do?

—Adena, age 11, 1983

Dear Adena,

Your letter tells us that you are feeling rather confused about how to handle your feelings. We agree with your mother that it is good to let your feelings out and to express yourself. Perhaps it is the way that you are expressing yourself that gets you into trouble rather than what you are saying. When you have something important to say, try to make sure that you say it in a way that will be clear and easily understood by others. It is very good to talk about your thoughts and feelings. That way they do not get all caught up inside of you and cause you problems. It is also important to be honest with people. By sharing your thoughts and feelings, people learn to know you and how you think.

If you feel that a contradiction exists at home, perhaps it would be a good idea to talk it over with Mom and Dad. They already encourage you to express your feelings, and we are sure that they would listen to you when you tell them about your problem. Maybe Mom and Dad could help you learn different ways of expressing yourself. At any event, they could certainly explain to you why there is a problem in communication.

We are sure that if you talk with your parents you will be able to work it out, Adena. As your mother has said, it is important to be able to express your feelings and have your feelings accepted.

Dear Highlights,

hi, i'm joss ever since I was 6 or 7, I've felt like my life would be much more comfortable if I decided to have . . . I dunno, aspects of both genders. the thing is, I don't know how to talk to my family about this.

I was born a girl and I've always accepted that I'm not very feminine, but I only feel right if I'm not addressed as a girl (or boy, really). my family is fairly religious, and because of that I'm afraid that telling them about my gender confusion will make them mad.

in the past I've had a few conversations with my mom about gender ambiguity, all of which have ended in her having suspicions about me and asking me "if [I'm] gay" in an angry tone. every time she asks me that, it sounds like she wants to hurt me even though she's told me that she has several lgbt friends.

even if my parents seem indifferent to it, they still want me to have a perfectly female lifestyle. I don't really feel comfortable wearing feminine clothing or "acting ladylike," but I feel if I tell them they'll look down on me and wish I were never born. I also tend to get made fun of a bit at school because people can't tell if I'm a boy or a girl.

I've done a lot of looking on the internet to find ways I can tell them without getting them mad, but I don't think I'm getting anything. I'm asking you guys because I've been reading highlights for as long as I can remember and it's made such a big impact on my life and all my choices. it's OK if you don't have a lot to say to me though, I'll understand.

—Joss, age 13, 2014

p.s.: my name isn't Joss, it's actually Joslyn.

Dear Joss,

We're glad you thought to write to us.

 If you don't feel comfortable talking to your parents just yet, you might first speak with another adult you feel comfortable with. This could be another relative, a guidance counselor at school, or a favorite teacher. One of these people might be able to offer you some helpful thoughts, as well as guidance about how to talk to your parents.

 It sounds as if you realize you'll have to talk to your parents at some point. It may be awkward and difficult, but in the end, you'll probably be glad to have shared your feelings with them. If it's too hard to talk to them in person, you might find it helpful to write your thoughts in a letter. You could start out by explaining how difficult it is for you to talk about this and let them know how much you love them. No matter what happens, we're sure they will continue to love you, Joss. You are a precious and beautiful person, and we know they'll always be glad you were born!

 We're sorry to hear that kids at school tease you sometimes. As you probably know, the best way to deal with this type of teasing is usually to ignore it. When you show that you're angry or upset, it then becomes a goal for the teasers to bother you even more. However, when you refuse to respond to it, it takes the fun out of the teasing.

 We hope this helps. Feel free to write to us whenever you need to.

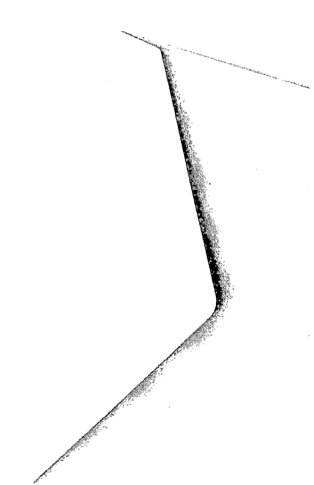

Letters About

Self-Improvement

I N OUR EXPERIENCE, KIDS ARE OFTEN INTERESTED IN
self-improvement. If the volume of letters we receive on the subject is
any indication, developing better personal habits or improving skills is
top of mind for many kids. Kids, when helped by caring adults, can
understand that trying their best is key to being happy and successful in
life. But they also worry about ridicule when they fail, and they worry about
disappointing the people who care about them.

Parents, of course, are expected to help shape their kids' behavior, and
kids, in general, try to cooperate. Younger kids are curious and need to test the
rules to understand limits. Another motivation of younger kids, who hold a
more literal understanding of rules, is to please the adults in their lives by
being obedient. But as kids grow, they want others to have a good impression
of them. That strong, human need for belonging kicks in and becomes a

primary motivator. They want to gain acceptance and positive attention from peers, especially, but also from parents and teachers.

Kids rarely write to object about their parents' or teachers' desire to see them change certain behaviors. Instead, they write for advice about how to create the needed change—how to abandon old ways and cement new, better habits. Amanda wrote to us in 1988 for tips on how to stop putting marker lids in her mouth, understanding it was unsafe. John, in 1997, wrote to say that he knew he had sloppy table manners and really wanted to learn to chew with his mouth closed. In 1998, Adam heard the message that his soda habit was out of control. He wanted to try to drink less soda. Christy, in 2003, wrote for help in breaking her habit of chatting online, which she wasn't allowed to do anyway.

Kids accept their parents' views about the habits they need to work on, even if they don't always fully grasp the why behind the what. Sometimes they are motivated by a simple desire to avoid punishment. Sometimes their motivation is a desire to please or be liked. These kids understand that trying to break personal habits frowned upon by others or considered off-putting will make them more pleasant to be around. They see the sense in addressing behaviors that put their health or safety at risk. As they work to do so, they discover how challenging self-discipline can be.

The habits that concern kids the most have been consistent over the years. They want to get better at finishing their household chores and their homework. They are concerned that they eat too many sweets. They often say they want to be more patient, more honest, less messy, and not so noisy. They worry about their screen time. In the 1980s, that meant watching television and playing video games, but today it may also mean watching too much

YouTube or engaging in too much social media. Some of the habits that concern kids may be self-correcting over time, but most will require kids to be intentional about addressing them.

Some children need help identifying healthy, realistic self-improvement goals. In 2015, Nolan wrote, "I play the piano. I love it except for one thing. If I mess up, I get mad at myself. I don't want to quit. Any advice?" In the same year, we heard from nine-year-old Tori, who wrote, "I have a stutter and I go to speech at school. Even when my speech therapist says it's getting better, I feel like it's just getting worse." In our replies to kids, we try to model for them the kind of compassionate self-talk we hope they can learn to use. We urge them to give up perfectionism as a goal and focus more on simply doing their best.

We urge them to give up perfectionism as a goal and focus more on simply doing their best.

Other kids have the opposite problem. They see the effect a poor habit is having on their lives, but they may need help understanding that they themselves will need to step up to create the change. Christopher, in 2007, wrote, "I really like playing video games, but my parents say I play too much. Can you help me not play so much?" Kids like Christopher and Angelina, who wrote to us in

2014, may need more explicit help with setting self-improvement goals that are challenging enough. We're not sure what Angelina was expecting to hear when she wrote to us that she thought she wanted to take on more responsibility, but didn't want to tell her parents. She worried they might give her a distasteful chore, such as changing the baby's diapers.

Our conversations with kids tell us that they often need help finding a healthy balance between self-acceptance and self-improvement. When we remind kids that they are lovable and loved just as they are, we help them put the right amount of focus on self-improvement. By urging them to stay focused on their effort and positive attitude, we can aid them in setting goals that will challenge but not frustrate them. We can help them learn how to be their own coaches.

Changing something we don't like about ourselves is hard, even for children. It requires persistent effort and fortitude. And for kids who are uncomfortable asking for help or who dislike feeling vulnerable, committing to change requires bravery. Rarely can kids have a private, internal epiphany as a prelude to intentionally working on themselves, as adults often can. Kids almost always have to embark on personal self-improvement by engaging the help of others.

Looking back over decades of letters, it's also clear that when we succeed in helping kids feel invested in becoming the best versions of themselves, it's a win-win. It's a win for kids, who feel empowered and are more open to receiving helpful advice. And it's a win for the caring adults, who want to see improvements but don't wish to relentlessly nag. Best of all is the long-term reward: better relationships for kids—and the increased likelihood of long-lasting, stable relationships as adults.

THE LETTERS

Dear Highlights,
I have a problem taking
care of the dog. I'm
supposed to take care of
her every day after school.
I usually forget to.
        —Beth, 1981

Dear Highlights,
My dad said I can get a pet
lizard in a few years but I have
to show that I'm responsible.
How can I do that?
        —Matthew, 2003

Dear Matthew,

It's great that you are thinking ahead about this. Many people get a pet because they know it will give them lots of enjoyment, but they don't plan for all of the responsibilities that go with having one. Your lizard will be dependent on you for all of its needs. It wouldn't be fair to take on a pet and then not give it the care it requires. Perhaps your dad has some things in mind that can help you show how responsible you are. For example, taking on chores and doing them regularly without being reminded will show that you are dependable.

Caring for a lizard requires daily responsibilities, such as feeding it, and less frequent chores, such as cleaning its cage. So perhaps you can take on daily and weekly tasks to show that you can keep up with both. You can check your school or public library for books about caring for lizards. Then you'll know what tasks you'll be responsible for when you get your pet.

The Reflection in the Mirror

The reflection in the mirror
a girl smiling back at me,

The reflection in the mirror . . .
the smile fades when the girl
remembers what she had done,

The reflection in the mirror . . .
a tear runs down her cheek,

The reflection in the mirror . . .
the tear now vanishes when she
realizes what she must do,

The reflection in the mirror . . .
the reflection vanishes as the girl
no longer has to face herself
but has to face someone else .

—Danielle, age 11, 1996

—Annalee, age 10, 2010

Too Much Television

When I come home the first thing I do is turn on the television and I watch television the whole day long and I forget to do everything that I have to do. My mother say's if I watch television too much My eye's will get bad. Is that true?

—Asha, age 7, 1985

Dear Highlights,
I always use the computer and can't stop. I feel that I'm not getting any smarter and the computer is warping my brain.
—P., 1978

Dear Highlights,
I'm playing on a Minecraft multi player server and have gottone addicted to it. Now I want to have a multiplayer server that anybody can join. Please help me get unaddicted.
—Anonymous, 2016

Dear Friend,

Just like many other people, it is likely that you use the computer out of habit. The only way to break a habit is to force yourself to do something different. A world of exciting and interesting activities is just waiting for you. Write a list of things you've always wanted to do, learn, make, or try. Refer to this list when you feel the urge to hop on the computer. Hop into a new sport, game, activity, or craft instead! Remember you control the computer. It doesn't control you.

Dear Highlights,
My brother left his email account on and I went on the computer and there was this folder that said "My Love" and I clicked on it and read his love e-mails. I feel really guilty but I don't know what to do!

PLEASE HELP!!!!

—Anonymous, 2014

Dear Friend,

We think it's important that you're listening to your feelings of guilt and discomfort, and we are proud of you for wanting to improve the situation.

It sounds as if your guilty feelings are telling you that you've done something wrong and it's time to apologize. Though we know it can be scary to admit to doing something wrong, the guilt and bad feelings you're experiencing now are worse than telling your brother the truth and dealing with his anger. His reaction will be based on the truth and will ultimately help you both work toward a better relationship.

The relationship between you and your brother is very special. We encourage you to do what you can to make that relationship as good as it can possibly be. You and he won't always agree. You will make mistakes, and you will sometimes act unwisely, but that's part of being human. Mistakes and even regrets such as you now have don't

make you a bad person. You are growing and learning. The good part is that our mistakes don't keep us from being wonderful people.

It is to your advantage to tell your brother what happened and apologize. You can even tell him that the guilt you've felt since snooping is not something you want to experience again. You can tell him earnestly that you have learned your lesson and will be even more conscious about respecting his privacy. He may get angry, but that will not last forever. He will still love you; we assure you.

A big part of growing up is learning to accept the consequences of your choices. You can take this experience and turn it into something good. It will help to build trust between you and your brother, and that's huge. And, you now know that hiding something you've done is not fun at all. This knowledge will help prevent you from doing a similar thing again.

Dear Editor,

I am 11 years old, and ever since I have been in shool, gym class has never been my bag. How can I improv? The kids don't think I'm too good, either.

—Steph, age 11, 1976

Dear Steph,

Not all of us can be equally good in everything. Try as hard as you can, but understand that there are others who are very good in gym class and may not be as good in other subjects, such as arithmetic. Just because we are not good in something does not mean that we should not keep on trying. It is probably good for us to have the experience of not being successful in everything we do. It helps us appreciate more those things that we are good at.

A Plan

Sitting in the car,
Thinking everything's crazy.
Headed to the house
To lie on the couch
To be lazy.
Going to get up in the morning
To go to school;
That's an everyday thing.
Seems to be cool.
I like my teacher.

She teaches me a lot.
She tries to help me
Be very smart.
I always have homework,
And I sometimes get behind.
But I'm going to start listening
And following my mind.
I promise to try
As hard as I can,
And that's Josh Taylor's plan!

—Josh, age 10, 2006

—Sybil, 1990

We had a play a few months ago at school, one of the songs we sang was Baby Baluga. For a long time I could not get it out of my head. Could you help me get it out of my head?

—Veronica, age 8, 1993

Dear Veronica,

There's a woman named Patty who works at Highlights. She hears songs in her head all the time. We asked her if she had any advice for you.

Patty says that it can be frustrating to hear the same song over and over. After a while, even a favorite song can get bothersome. So she pretends that the song is on a radio station, and in her mind, she changes the station. She hums a few bars of the new song in her head and concentrates on it. The new song replaces the old one. Then, when she gets tired of that song a few days later, she changes it. Sometimes, though, a song on the radio or a commercial jingle works its way into her head, and that's the tune she hears.

Patty usually gets enjoyment from hearing music all the time. When she wants to relax, she tries to imagine a slow, soothing song. When she wants to get some work done, she imagines a song with a quick tempo.

Patty used to think that everyone heard music in their head, and she was amazed to find out that not many people do. So try not to let this bother you too much. Instead, think of it as your special gift. You could try learning to play an instrument or joining a choir. Maybe the music in your head is trying to tell you that music can be an important part of your life.

Dear Highlights, I'm 10 yrs. old. I've been having problems with myself I seem to have any patience I'm always getting screamed at. I don't no if it's a stage or what! Help! Help! Miserable,

—Marisol, age 10, 1982

Dear Marisol,

It is often very hard to have patience, especially at your age, when you want things to happen right away. You do learn to have more patience as you grow older. It takes a lot of practice and determination. You will probably learn how to control yourself better as you grow.

You told us that you seem to be getting yelled at a lot. It would probably be a good idea to sit down with Mom or Dad or whoever is yelling at you and try to talk about the problem. You could ask what you could do to make things better.

It is very important to talk things over. Together with your parents, you might find a solution that makes everyone happier.

Dear Highlights,
I am having a real problem of bossing my friends around. And they get mad. So I wondered if you could give me some advice.

—Amy, 1996

Dear Amy,

Recognizing that there may be a problem and seeking help are good first steps in making changes.

Ask friends to remind you when you're being bossy. They probably will appreciate that you are working to improve and will be glad to help. You might agree on a signal they could make when you boss them, such as pulling gently on their ears. When you see the signal, you can stop and think of a different way to talk to them.

Also, think about what you are feeling when you boss people. You may be upset about something else or feel impatient because you want your own way. Maybe you think that your way is best for everyone—but not everyone may agree with that. Ask a trusted adult to help you find ways to deal with those feelings instead of taking them out on others.

Dear Highlights,
I've been struggling to have a better attitude about daily circumstances. How can I become a more positive person?

—Gus, 2018

Dear Gus,

One thing that can help change your attitude is gratitude! Try making a list of all you are grateful for. Set aside a few minutes each day to add to the list. The more you think about the good things in your life, the less you'll focus on things that bother you. It's also important to accept that things won't always go your way. Rather than getting frustrated, tell yourself that it's OK, and make a new plan. Think about how you can move forward. Try to have a sense of humor about situations you can't change.

Dear HighHights,

I owe people money and I either don't
have enough money or I forget. PLEASE
HELP!

—Charlie, age 9, 2007

Dear Charlie,

The first step in making sure that you pay back money is to set a goal. Perhaps you'll want to make a chart that shows what you owe to each person. It might help to choose a date by which you'll pay back each amount that you owe. Make your deadlines realistic, not too soon and not too far in the future.

Next, make a list of things you might do to earn money. With a parent's permission, you might do odd jobs in your neighborhood, such as cutting grass, walking dogs, or checking mail for neighbors who are away on vacation. You might also ask your parents if you can do extra chores around the house. Ask your friends what kinds of things they do to make money. Add their ideas to your list.

As you earn money, try the "rule of thirds" for saving. Put a third of the money in your pocket to spend, a third in a piggy bank or savings account for things you'd like to buy in the future, and a third to repay what you owe to others. If you have a hard time saving to repay what you owe, ask your parents to hold the money for you, and then get it back when you've earned enough to repay what you borrowed.

One other thing you might want to consider: If you don't borrow money, you won't have to worry about paying it back. Although it can seem difficult at first to wait to buy things you want, it's a great habit to develop. "Debt" is easy to get into and not as easy to get out of. If you learn to save for what you want now, as an adult you'll likely be very responsible with the money you earn.

Dear Highlights,
I have been saving money in the bank for two years. What do you think I ought to do with it? My grandfather says I should buy stocks.

—Stephen, age 8, 1998

Dear Stephen,

We think it's great that you are saving some money. But we don't think we're the people who should help you figure out what to do with your savings. We suggest that you talk to your parents about your question. You might begin by telling them what you want to do with the money. Then listen to what they say. They may have some great ideas for you. We're sure they will want to know what you are thinking and that they will be proud to know that you are being thoughtful and responsible about such an important matter.

Dear Highlights,
I am nine years old. We moved from one town to another. All of our friends live in my old town, but I never have time to write letters to my friends. What should I do?

—Jennifer, 1979

Dear Jennifer,

We can understand that moving to a new place has kept you busy and that you might not find time to write letters to all your friends. We hope you will take time to at least send them some short greetings. Why not make some postcards and drop one in the mail each week? Set yourself a schedule to do that. We hope you are making new friends and enjoying your new school.

Dear Highlights,
    My problem is that it's
not easy for me to keep a secret.
Like when _____ told me that
_____ been absent because
his father died, she told me not
to tell a soul; well, I did. I told
_____ (who also gets Highlights) and
I'm afraid they might tell and
_____ will kill me? Can you help
me?

—Molly, 1997

Dear Molly,

You took the first step already when you realized that telling other people's secrets is not appropriate. You must watch what you say. One way to do this is to tell yourself that you won't say anything unless you slowly count to ten before you speak. This will give you time to consider what you are about to say.

You might talk with your friend and tell her how her secret slipped out. She might be annoyed at first, but she would be more annoyed if she found out from someone else. Tell her that you would like to learn to keep secrets better. She may appreciate the effort you want to make and might be able to give you some helpful suggestions on how to go about it.

Even if some remarks slip out, it always helps to apologize immediately to the person who might be upset. People can be forgiving when someone is truly sorry about what they have done. Sometimes it also helps to write things down in a diary. That would be like telling your diary the secret instead of telling another person.

Most new habits take time to form, so try to be patient with yourself. Remember that you have the best intentions at heart.

Dear Highlights,

I had an obsession with chewing gum. In other words, I chewed way more gum than my stomach would like. So I closed the gum container and put it away and didn't chew any gum for three or four days. Now I only eat one piece a day. Sometimes none.

—Anonymous, 1979

Dear Friend,

Thank you for your message. It's great that you broke your habit! That takes a lot of mental strength and determination. We're proud of you for recognizing that you had a problem and then taking clear steps to change your behavior. We encourage you to keep sticking with your new plan. If you would like to stop chewing gum altogether, try finding something to distract you from wanting to chew. A good idea is to keep a water bottle with you at all times. When you get the urge to chew, take a sip of water. It not only occupies you but keeps you hydrated. Your parents might also have some good ideas for you.

I Am Somebody

I am somebody
And I want to be—
Not because I'm black
But because I'm me.

I must strive every day
To be a better person to know,
And in order to be successful
I must work at it so I'll grow.

I surely want to grow
But not just in height.
I must improve my mind
And start thinking right.

I realize though
That I must improve my worth.
You get very little for nothing—
That's how it is on Earth.

So I'm striving to be better,
And one day they'll all see
That I am somebody—
And it's because I'm me.

—Elisha, age 9, 1997

—Aoife, age 9, 2019

picky eater
I hate eating stuff
like sweet potatos
what should i do

—Tim, age 6, 1999

Dear Tim,

You might talk with your parents about how you feel and about how they feel. Together you might come up with some ideas about different ways in which foods might be more appealing to you. For instance, if you like vegetable soup, perhaps your parent could cut sweet potatoes into small pieces and cook them in the soup.

As they grow older, many children begin to like foods they didn't like before, particularly if they have eaten small amounts of them in the past. Eating small amounts of food that you don't like gives your taste buds the chance to develop and become accustomed to flavors so that, eventually, you may enjoy such foods.

One way of helping you to eat foods you don't like is to think about the nutrition they're providing for you. You might discuss with your parents how certain foods can help you grow in a strong and healthy way. Then, when you're eating those foods, concentrate on the good they are doing for you.

We hope this helps.

Dear Highlights,

I am unsatisfied with my life. After having grown up watching Disney movies and reading magazines (like yours) about these kids who do amazing things and have perfect lives, I can't take it anymore! My life is boring, pointless and unhappy! I wish I could do amazing things like your "Gallant Kids" do, and more than that I've alwasy felt like I'm special, and I know everyone is special, but I feel like there's something different about ME. Like I'll discover one day I have magic powers or something. I've always talked to animals, sutffed animals, rocks, trees, inanimate objects. I talk to myself more than I talk to other people and even my closest friends and family really don't understand the bounds of my imagination. I want MORE from my life. I don't want to be just part of the common crowd. I know this sounds stupid, but it's the truth. I believe in magic and everything and I'm tired of people acting like I'm stupid for it! I just have a huge imagination. So what's the bottom line? The bottom line is, how can I make my life magical?

—Farah, 2016

Dear Farah,

It's always good to ask for help when you don't know what to do. You said that you are looking for ways to make your life magical, exciting, and special. What a wonderful goal to set for yourself!

There are a few things that we noticed about your message. The first is that you started by comparing yourself to other people, including characters in movies and stories. Though we know it's easy to slip into comparisons with others—and that it's very natural and sometimes helpful to draw inspiration from other people in our lives—we encourage you to stay focused on you and your own personal goals, ambitions, strengths, and ideas as you think about your life. It's easy to (wrongly) think that other people's lives are perfect, easy, or effortless. But really, we overlook the fact that everyone has challenges, everyone has weaknesses, and everyone works hard and has setbacks.

Instead of comparing yourself to friends and family or characters in movies and stories, look inward. You might start with some serious personal thought. What would make your life more magical to you? What are the best, most exciting ways for you to use your big imagination? How would your special, unique set of strengths lend themselves to your very own "Gallant Kids" type of project? What hobbies, activities, new skills, or new experiences seem most magical, exciting, and special to you?

Dear Highlights,

Sometimes I cuss (say bad words) when my grandparents are not around. I want to stop cussing

P.S. I'm NOT telling my grandparents that I cuss.

—Jake, age 9, 2013

I AM SAYING SORRY
TO MUCH CAN
YOU HELP?

—Miles, age 8, 2014

Dear Jake,

We're glad you recognize the need to stop cussing. It's good to be aware of personal shortcomings because it means you can continue to become the best person you can possibly be!

One way to stop is to replace the bad words with good or silly words. For example, instead of swearing, you could say "rutabaga" or "parsnip." If you do this enough, you will hopefully break the habit of swearing.

If you ever do feel as though you can talk to your grandparents about this habit, we're sure they would have some ideas of how to help you stop. We all make mistakes, but it's recognizing those mistakes and learning from them that show maturity. We think your grandparents would be proud of you for the choice you are making. You can also talk to your parents or another trusted adult, who may have more thoughts to share with you.

Dear Miles,

It's good to say sorry when you are at fault for something. However, it's also good to recognize whether or not you need to apologize. You shouldn't feel the need to take on responsibility for things that aren't your fault.

Rather than saying, "I'm sorry," perhaps you can think of another phrase to say, such as, "That's too bad." Or sometimes just say nothing at all. We suggest you think for a moment before speaking and decide whether or not you need to say sorry.

If you haven't yet, we encourage you to talk to your parents about this. They may have some advice for you on how to handle this situation.

Dear Leah,

Some people are naturally louder or quieter than others. If you make a lot of noise walking around, you could make it a game: Stomp like a giant, making as much noise as you can, and then walk around as quietly as a cat. Practice being as soft and careful as a cat more often than being a giant!

If you know you speak loudly, try to match the volume of your voice to others around you. Rather than interrupting or talking over others in a conversation, wait until they finish speaking to share your thoughts. Before you share an opinion with someone, take the time to ask yourself what your opinion will add to the conversation. Are you sharing a new idea? Will your opinion help the other person make a decision? Will it upset the other person? If your opinion contributes to the conversation in a meaningful way, then it's OK to share it when it's your turn. If your opinion will upset the other person, you may want to keep it to yourself.

If you accidentally interrupt someone while you're trying to break your habit, apologize as soon as you can. Don't be discouraged by mistakes. It will get easier as time passes.

2 Year Arizona

I have rather a bad habit.
I'm really noisy.

And I alwase have an opinion.
and There not always good.
And I lwase have to stick in my two cents.

—Leah, age 8, 2017

I Love My Piano

I love my piano.
But some days when my mom says
it's time to practice,
I just feel like screaming!
   kicking!
   crying!
   plugging my ears!
   hiding my music books!
   BANGING ON THE KEYS!
But then I start to practice, and then,
I can't STOP!
I LOVE MY PIANO!

—Jessica, age 8, 1991

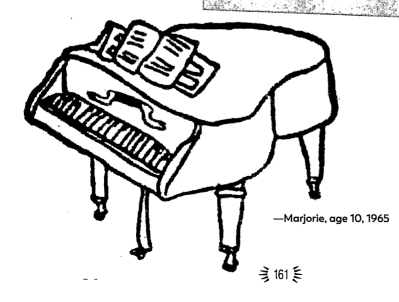

—Marjorie, age 10, 1965

Hopes & Dreams

AT HIGHLIGHTS, WE BELIEVE THAT A CHILD'S HOPE or dream is never too small to consider. Often when adults talk about hopes and dreams as they relate to young kids, they are thinking of the aspirations that parents hold for their children. But all children, even young kids, have their own hopes and dreams. Kids have been writing to us for decades about their desire to do good, their belief in themselves, and their optimistic view of a future world.

Sometimes a child's expressed dream represents a fleeting interest—a snapshot of a moment in their childhood or a mere flirtation with a specific idea. But often, children's dreams can indicate the direction their interests and abilities will take them, which is why we at Highlights always try to be supportive and encouraging as kids "try on" possibilities. Even the dreams that may seem silly to adults can be important stepstones to a dream or a goal that is more meaningful or achievable. The child who writes us today with a fervent desire to be a YouTube influencer (or in the 1980s or 1990s, a TV or movie star) may choose a different career later, but perhaps one that still allows them to showcase strengths, such as creativity, a talent for predicting trends, or an ability to communicate in an entertaining way.

Even the dreams that may seem silly to adults can be important stepstones to a dream or a goal that is more meaningful or achievable.

Some children start with a big, meaningful aspiration, but struggle to develop a dream that shows them a way to move forward. In 1983, Paul wrote, "When I grow up, I want to help the needy. Do you have any suggestions?" In 2014, an ambitious reader wanting to have an impact on the world wrote, "I am the kind of kid who wants to do something BIG someday, like finding talking animals or convince the President of something. But where does the adventure begin?"

How can we adults fail to be inspired by their earnest desire to do good and by their belief in their own potential?

Kids who dare to dream often see a world that is larger than themselves —a better world. They write to share their yearnings for a world that is kinder, more peaceful, and more empathetic. In times of war, we receive letters from kids who want to be peacemakers or to work to promote mutual understanding across the globe. In 1969, Patricia wrote to say that her dream was to join the

Peace Corps when she grew up and asked us to tell her more about it. In the early 2000s, many kids sent us letters and original poems expressing their concern about conflict in the Middle East.

As we settled more deeply into the Digital Age, our mailbag continued to reflect kids' interest in current events and their growing feeling of empowerment. Kids can be surprisingly clear-eyed, seeming to understand that hope alone is not a strategy for making the world a better place. Some letters reflect an increased interest in careers related to STEM and an ever-growing understanding that science and technology can create a path to solving many of the world's challenges. More exposure to the news seems to have awakened in some kids an interest in activism, not unlike what we saw in reader mail from the 1960s. Although kids may not be thinking about it exactly like this, these dreamers are considering not only what they want to be when they grow up but also who they want to be. Over the decades, and particularly in more recent years when kids have felt freer to speak their minds, the children who write to us amaze us with their sense

Kids who dare to dream often see a world that is larger than themselves— a better world.

of altruism and their wish to contribute to a greater good.

In our responses to young writers who share hopes and dreams, we try to affirm their desire to grow, to be better, and to do good. We want them to know that they have agency—that they can choose their dreams and are free to act on them. We try to dispel any preconceived ideas that are limiting, such as racial discrimination, cultural differences, learning ability, and gender stereotyping. When Sally wrote to us in 1971, sharing her dream of becoming a doctor, she asked, "Would that be a good profession for a girl?" Similarly, in 2003, when Alexis, who dreamed of being an animal keeper, was told by her brother to stick to a "girl job," we assured both readers that women can succeed in any career if they give it their best effort. (Worth noting: We've been talking about sex discrimination with girls for 50 years and still do!)

When kids ask for help overcoming obstacles in their path, we remind them that when they work hard and try their best, they show themselves and others that they are capable of doing great things. Sometimes the obstacles are a lack of money or lack of how-to information. Commonly, there is a lack of support from others. In 2004, a reader wrote to

> **We remind them that when they work hard and try their best, they show themselves and others that they are capable of doing great things.**

say his dreams were crushed when his father disapproved of his plan to become "a YouTuber." How can he disapprove, the reader asked, "when he doesn't even know what YouTube is?" Ashley, in 1976, wrote about her wish to go to Harvard and become an architect, but she said everyone was laughing and saying she wasn't smart enough. Our replies include suggestions for how the writer might think about their perceived obstacles and the idea that they look for a mentoring adult.

But the reply we gave to ten-year-old Jessica in 1997 contains the idea that we hope every young dreamer takes to heart and holds with them forever. She wrote: "Dear Highlights, I have always wanted to fly, but I know I never will fly. What can I do to stop dreaming of flying?" Unsure if she aspired to be a pilot or if she was harboring a fantasy of flying like a bird, we covered both possibilities: "We hope you never stop hoping to fly, Jessica. Sometimes even the most daring of dreams come true."

May every child dream of flying high.

THE LETTERS

Dear Editor,

I love animals and wildlife. I would like to know what jobs a woman can get working with animals and wildlife. Also, I would like to know what training she should take to help her get an outdoor job. What classes do you recommend I work hard on in Junior High to help me get a job working in wildlife?

—Lisa, age 12, 1976

Dear Highlights,
I've thought it over and I want to be a fireman. What do you think of that job for a girl?

—Donna, 1977

Dear Donna,

How nice it is that you are already thinking about what you want to be when you are grown! By exploring different occupations now, you will be better prepared when you are older and must make a final decision.

Being a firefighter is certainly important work that would be interesting as well as challenging. As long as you are able to meet all of the qualifications, there is no reason why it isn't a good occupation for a girl to consider.

Dear Highlights,

I signed up to play tackle football this fall. I'm actually decent at the sport, but I'm the only girl, and that could mean I will be underestimated. How can I prove that I am good enough to play quarterback?

–Emma, 2016

Dear Emma,

Playing football this fall sounds very exciting for you as well as for other girls who might be interested in playing football.

People will think what they're going to think, Emma, and you can't control that. Some people may underestimate you, but you must not focus your attention on that. Rather, simply go out there each day, play your best, show that you're willing to learn, and be a good teammate. Be supportive of the other players just as you hope they will be toward you. Little by little, day by day, you will prove yourself. That is true as you play football as well as any other endeavor you take on. You must maintain an I-can-do-it attitude.

We think you're going to have a tremendously exciting fall! Be sure to share your concerns with your parents, coach, or other trusted adult, as well. They may have some helpful suggestions for you.

Dear Highlights,
I am a real lover of science and someday hope to discover the cure for cancer. I was wondering if you knew any places where I could find some books or equipment I could use to help me.

—Linda, 1979

Dear Highlights,
I would like to become a nuclear physicist. Could you please answer these questions for me.
1. Which college should I go to?
2. How many years of college should I need? 3. Who would employ me? 4. In what part of the country would I work? 5. How much would my salary be? 6. What high school courses should I take?

—Stephen, 1967

Dear Stephen,

We're glad you want to be a nuclear physicist. Any high-standard college should be good for you to enter. You would need to have at least four years of college with high grades, plus three or four more years of graduate study. It is most important that in high school you make good grades in all of your courses, especially English, mathematics, and science. Complete all the math and science courses your advisor suggests. Take his or her advice on your courses and on the choice of a graduate school. It is too many years away to suggest where you might be employed or what your salary might then be. But there should be no problem in finding a position and earning a good living.

Growing Up

When I grow up I want to be
So many different things—
A writer, a poet, a movie star,
A lovely girl who sings.

When I grow up I want to be
What I think and see.
When you grow up, be yourself
And be what you want to be.

—Jackie, age 11, 2003

—Kim, age 10

Dear Hilights,

I'm 11 and I am trying

to make a company to sell

wooden trinkets!

I Don't have enough time
to make the website.

~~————————~~

what should I Do?
sinserly,

—Felix, age 11, 2015

Dear Highlights,
I want to start a
bread bissness but I
don't know how. My
parents say I need
to buy my own
things for baking
such as flour, yeast
and other things, it
sounds like a lot of
money! Please help!
—Devorah, 2015

Dear Deborah,

You sound like an ambitious person!

It's true that starting and running a business can be expensive. Perhaps it would help if you sit down with your parents and make a list of things you would need and estimate their cost. Once you do this, you will have a better idea of just how much money you'll need.

Many entrepreneurs (people who start their own business) earn money for their start-up costs by doing other jobs. With your parents' permission, you might offer to do some jobs, such as vacuuming, sweeping, dusting, helping with yard work, and so on, for close neighbors or relatives. If there is a friend or relative near you who has young children, you might offer to play with the children while their parents do other work around the house. Of course, you will need to speak to your parents about this idea first.

You might ask your friends for ideas, too. You could also ask a librarian to recommend books about kids who have started their own businesses.

Best wishes—and happy baking.

Dear Highlights,
When I grow up I don't want to be known for my riches. I want to be known for my kindness and for discovering something which would be very useful to the world. I am going to be a chemist. I already have a head start in the world of chemistry, and I know I won't change my mind when I grow up.

—Bruce, 1964

If I Could Change the Way Things Are

If I could change the way things are, I'd . . .
Make people understand me better,
Get rid of boredom and frustration,
Take away my bad temper and teach me
    patience,
Make life seem more challenging and fun,
Make it so that no one ever failed.
If I could change the way things are, I'd . . .
Eliminate crime and gangs and wars,
Stop all kinds of fighting everywhere,
Make people be fair,
Stop teasing and cruelty,
Stop lies.
I guess I would try to make the world more
    like God must have wanted it to be,
Before we all came and messed it up.

—Ryan, age 10, 1997

—Rory, age 10, 2015

Dear Highlights,

My friends and I are in a band. We wrote three song lyrics and we're ready to make our sample C.D. Two problems though. First, we have a tune to the lyrics, but no music. And second, who do we contact, telling we want to make a C.D.

I know this isn't like a problem at school or home, so I won't mad if you can't answer it.

—Rochelle, age 10, 1998

Dear Rochelle,

We're glad to hear that you and your friends are in pursuit of a creative endeavor. It will be wise to seek the support and advice of adults who have your best interests at heart. Be sure that all your parents fully understand what you want to do.

You might check with your school's music teacher about music for your lyrics or find a music student or teacher who would be willing to write out the musical score for the tune you have in mind. This service may not be free. Then it will be necessary to practice the music until the vocal arrangement is near perfect.

We don't have contacts to suggest for making CDs. Your school music teacher might also suggest places or people to contact. Ask the reference librarian at your local library for help. There might be contacts on the internet, but these need to be checked out thoroughly to avoid scams. That's why it's especially important for you to have adult help that you can trust.

No matter what happens, Rochelle, continue to enjoy music, whether playing in the band, singing, or being an enthusiastic listener. Music will bring joy to your life.

Jan 3 2,000

Dear Highlights, I'm thinking about my career. I really want to be a basketball player but on the other hand I want to be a football player, What should I do?

P.S. Can you please respond by a letter? Thanks!

—Adam, age 11, 2000

Dear Adam,

Isn't it great that you don't have to make this decision today? It's good that you're thinking about your future, and it's also good that you have more than one interest. You have many years yet in which you can participate in many sports and other activities. As you grow and enjoy new experiences, you will discover the areas in which you excel. You will also become aware of the activities which most interest you.

For now, we encourage you to enjoy playing both basketball and football. You will benefit from learning the techniques of both games, about self-discipline and team cooperation, as well as about building friendships and just having fun. There will be plenty of time later on to focus your energies on just one goal.

Dear Highlights,
Me and my friend are spys and Detectives.
We can not find a mystry but however we
do find some but they are always getting
Solved. We need help and we need it fast!

—Lucy and Amanda, 1999

Dear Lucy and Amanda,

We think it's great that you are interested in solving mysteries. Being a good detective requires critical thinking skills that can be helpful in a number of areas throughout life. Since you are having trouble finding mysteries, why don't you create some of your own? The two of you could take turns creating mysteries for the other to solve—hiding clues in different places around your houses, or even around the neighborhood, if your parents say it's OK. You may also want to ask parents, siblings, or other people to create mysteries for you.

Most libraries have a collection of mystery stories for kids to read and enjoy. There are also board games that rely on detective skills to win. You may want to talk to your parents about taking you to the library or purchasing a mystery board game.

Be careful when working on real-life mysteries, and be sure to clear them with parents first. If you think there might be danger involved, tell an adult and leave the solving up to them.

Hope

Hope is like the stars, shining bright far
   far away, yet very close at hand.
Hope is like tomorrow—you know it's close
   but don't know what's in store.
Hope is like the ocean, the oldest thing on
   earth, very alive, always moving,
   always changing, surviving time itself.
Everyone has hope, babies are born with hope.
I've stumbled across hope in crowded walkways,
I've seen hope in newspapers, I've listened to hope.
HOPE IS EVERYWHERE

—Kenneth, age 13, 1985

—Briana, age 10, 2008

Career

My parents want me to be a Lawer when I grow up. But I love art. I want to be an artist. I love sketching with pencils, but I'm to afraid to tell my parents that, I hint, but it dosen't work. Can you help me?

—Emily, age 9, 1993

Dear Emily,

Your parents may be urging you to be a lawyer because you display some character traits that would make you a successful lawyer. Perhaps you are good at speaking, can think fast, and have a good sense of what is right and wrong. Or, perhaps your mother or father is a lawyer and they would like for you to follow in their footsteps.

Either way, we're sure your parents realize that you are still young to be choosing your career. Since you enjoy art and sketching with pencils, then we would suggest you continue pursuing your artistic interests. It is usually true that the things we enjoy doing the most are the things we are good at. We think it is likely that your parents' biggest desire is for you to have a happy childhood and adult life, doing what you enjoy.

If you still feel uncomfortable about your parents' career choice for you, you might want to talk to them about it. We think that will help you feel better.

Dear Highlights,
I have grown very interested in the blind and deaf. I've learned sign language and braille. I want to help teach the blind and deaf.

—Rebecca, 1983

Dear Rebecca,

We think that your ambition to teach deaf and blind students is an admirable goal. You already have made a good start by learning sign language and braille. Right now, you can prepare best by studying very hard in school. You will have to learn a great deal in high school and later in college to become a teacher of the handicapped.

Dear Highlights,

I want to make some money so I can get a computer and computer equipment. I want to do this by working on computers. I like working on computers, so I want to make money with them. I thought up a motto—We can't fix it, we don't charge it. I know a person who would like computer tutoring, and people sometimes need help doing things with their computer. I would charge quite a bit less than professionals, too. But nobody except me and my parents believes I can do these things. My mom says to wait until I'm older, but I want some money now. I get five dollars a week allowance, but this is not enough. Can you help?

—Chad, 1997

Dear Chad,

We think it's wonderful that you want to work hard to reach your goals. You might want to talk to your parents about the situation. Politely explain your feelings. Listen to what they have to say. They may not change their minds about things, but at least you will have a better understanding of their views.

If your parents still think you should wait to begin your business, you might want to use the extra time to develop your plans. You could begin to work out details such as how people will know about your business. How will they get in touch with you? What will your hours be? Will you still have enough time for schoolwork? You might want to go to the library and check out some books about starting your own business. This will help you to prepare for the future when your parents give you permission to go ahead with your plans.

When the Time Comes

When the time comes to leave—
Leave my best friends,
Leave my teachers—
I wonder if I will ever grow up to
be me.
Grow up to be what I want to be,
Grow up to be a famous poem-writer.
I want to be able to face wrong things.
I want to be myself.

—Raynard, age 10, 1972

—Brooklyn, age 5, 2015

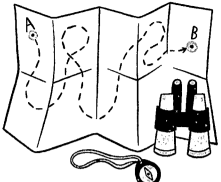

Dear Highlights,
I want to go on an adventure or a journey by myself and explore good stuff. But I don't want to get caught going outside!
—Anonymous, 2013

Dear Friend,

Having an adventure or going on a journey does sound like fun! But you're right that it wouldn't be a good idea to do something that you're not supposed to do.

We suggest that you talk to your parents about where you are and are not allowed to go when you go outside. Then figure out where you can go to have a great adventure within those limits. Or perhaps ask one of your parents to come with you on your adventures. We're sure they're just concerned about your safety. So, it's important to discuss these rules and make sure you're clear about them.

Good luck exploring!

Dear Highlights,
When I get older, I want to be a congresslady but I don't know how to start.
—Tracy, 1985

Dear Tracy,

Serving in Congress would be a great way to have an interesting career and help others, too. To be a good congresswoman, you will need to have a broad background, and you will have to know how to work with others. So do your best in your schoolwork. Learn all you can about history and geography. Try to become involved in activities in your community, too. Your parents could also help you find local addresses for your state's senators and representatives, or you can write to them at the House of Representatives or the Senate in Washington, D.C. If you write and explain what you would like to know, they will probably give you some useful advice.

Dear Highlights,

I really hate crimes. I keep hearing about people committing them on TV, and it really bugs me. Is there anything I could do to help with our crime problem?

—Serena, 2012

Dear Serena,

Stopping crimes in action is a job best left for the police. But preventing crimes from happening is just as important. And the best way you can do that is by being a good citizen yourself. Your good example will hopefully influence your friends and family to make similar life decisions. We know it may not seem like much, but one person does make a difference.

Remember that while there are many crimes in the world, there are also many good things happening. Try to focus on these good things, and we think you'll find that you are happier. In the news, they tend to focus on stories that involve crime and other disturbing topics, but there are good stories as well. Yesterday, there was an article about a boy who won $1,000, and he gave all the money to his two-year-old neighbor, who is fighting leukemia.

We try to emphasize these good deeds in *Highlights* in our "Gallant Kids" section. We hope you will look for that in our issues. There are many kids doing wonderful things to help their communities.

Dear Highlights,
When I grow up I would like to be like John Fitzgerald Kennedy. I would love to join the Peace Corps. The story of John Fitzgerald Kennedy told about his humor and his great love for his country. Even though we lost him, Americans won't forget the love he had for our country.

—Kathryn, 1964

Dear Sherri,

Becoming a computer technician would be a fine career. If you do your best at your studies now, you will have a good chance of reaching that goal.

Although designing a force field might be a good idea, it would be even better to work to prevent nuclear war in the first place. There are many groups and organizations that are against such a war. Look for one in your area. If you work at stopping nuclear war now, you may be able to spend your time as a computer technician designing other things.

Dear Highlights,

I would like to tell you my one and only wish. I've always wanted to be in the Olympics and someday I'm going to get there. My goal is swimming. I work hard. I am a very athletic person. I have many ribbons and medals and many trophies. I have the highest award that anyone could get—a silver spike with my name engraved on it.

—Gretchen, 1979

Dear Gretchen,

We think you should be proud of yourself for your athletic achievements. You say you work hard. Athletics take a great deal of work and a great deal of willpower to stick to a training program. Our best wishes to you.

I am Eric

I am a dreamer and an inventor
I wonder if I could grow wings
I hear the moon saying good-night to everybody
  on earth
I see the sun waving good-bye when night comes
I want to fly
I am a dreamer and an inventor

I pretend to fly through the sky
I feel my mom kissing me good-night
I touch the moon
I worry when my brother holds my shells
  over cement
I cry when everything goes wrong
I am a dreamer and an inventor

—Michael, age 9, 1996

I understand there is not peace on earth
I say that magic is real
I dream that there is a place where only
  the truth and good are
I try to fly
I am a dreamer and an inventor

—Eric, age 9, 1991

Dear Highlights,
Do you have any ideas about how to get a job? I'm 10 yr. old and I'm trying to make money for college. I've all ready make $20 and I've got 8yr intell college.
—Jeremiah, 2019

Dear Jeremiah,

It's great that you have saved $20 toward college, Jeremiah! Looking toward the future and saving responsibly shows that you are serious about your goal.

You might ask your parents if there are some jobs around your house that you could become responsible for. With their permission, you might offer the same services to close neighbors or relatives.

To think of more ideas, it might help to start by making a list of all your skills and interests. Write down everything you can think of, even if you're not sure how it will help. Then look at your finished list and brainstorm ways to turn those interests into jobs.

Whatever job you may be given, we encourage you to do it on time and to the best of your ability, even if you don't like the job. Develop a good attitude toward it. A positive attitude and a willingness to work hard will be your biggest assets throughout life. As you prove that you are both capable and responsible, more opportunities are likely to come your way.

Dear Highlights,
I would like to live in an igloo without any luxuries. I think Americans have too many luxuries. Do you think this would be healthy for an eleven year old to attempt?
—Amy, 1984

Dear Amy,

We think it is fine that you are concerned about all the luxuries that we take for granted. People in many parts of the world could not even imagine life with all the luxuries that we enjoy. We do not think that trying to live in an igloo by yourself would be a wise thing to do, though. Find out whether Scouts in your area have a wilderness camping program or whether there is an Outward Bound or similar wilderness school you could go to. Trying to live very simply can help us to learn more about our inner strengths, but first you need to learn the skills that are needed for wilderness survival.

Societal Concerns & Events

KIDS ARE SO DEEPLY FOCUSED ON FAMILY, friends, and school that it might be easy to underestimate their awareness of the world's big issues. Many school-aged children, however, have the ability to look outside of themselves and realize that they are a part of something bigger. The letters kids send to us about complex world problems reveal their willingness to learn about them—as well as their wish to help.

Kids learn about real-world issues in a variety of ways. Some of what they know comes from the news, conversations with peers, social media, or the internet. The information they glean in these ways may be inaccurate, devoid of context, or beyond their comprehension, causing anxiety or fear. Kids who learn about these difficult subjects in school often fare better, seeming more informed and hopeful. And, of course, one of the primary ways kids acquire knowledge of the world's problems is by listening to their parents, whose thoughts significantly shape kids' own nascent opinions.

Whatever their source of information, most kids are aware that many serious problems plague the world. Some problems strike a chord with them more than others, and the issues they write to us about the most have remained consistent over the years. These include animal rights, conservation, climate change, hunger and homelessness, war, and terrorism. (Sadly, we haven't made much progress on these problems.)

The response of some children to an issue they care about can be visceral. For them, hearing about any suffering, tragedy, or threat awakens a driving curiosity to learn more, and the empathy they express humbles us. Kids like these are fervent, and they feel an urgent need to help address the problem. In 1998, ten-year-old Tanya said that every time she goes into the meat aisle at the grocery store, she thinks about the animals that were slaughtered so we can eat meat. "How can I prevent that?" she wanted to know. Suzy, in 2011, wrote: "Ever since that giant earthquake hit Japan, I feel awful for the people living there. I've already donated money, but I don't feel like I'm doing enough. Any ideas about other ways I can help Japan?"

When others fail to be supportive or don't demonstrate the same level of fervor, these young activists feel frustrated. In 1982, Padma wrote: "I told my parents, sisters, and brother that they should learn to conserve energy and water. But they don't seem to listen! They save water by not letting it run. But they don't turn off the lights! Up until today, I went from room to room to turn off lights, but I'm tired of doing it. What should I do?" In a 1995 letter, Crystal wrote: "I'm really concerned about the Earth . . . I've tried to recycle cans and newspapers, but my parents just end up throwing it away. What should I do?"

Kids seem to know that understanding a problem is where helping begins, and they are eager to learn. Over the years, kids have looked to us for validating what they think they know and for help filling in the knowledge gaps. In 1976, for example, Julie wrote, "I love animals very much. I would like to know how I can help endangered species."

Today, of course, many kids look to the internet for that kind of basic information. But they still turn to us for answers to more difficult questions. In 2017, Emmy asked us if water was a human right. In 2018, Lily wrote to us about her own and her sister's distress after reading that tigers are endangered. "But how much can two girls do to make a difference?" In 2002, Stu asked if it was wrong to hate Osama bin Laden. "My teacher said if you love Osama bin Laden, something is wrong with you," he wrote. "But the Bible tells us to love your enemies. I don't like him or hate him yet. Not until I get my answer."

Unfortunately, some kids' awareness of the world's dark side is a result of feeling its impact more directly. After Margaret's father was deployed to Bosnia in 2001 on a peacemaking mission, she said she was "going berserk without him." She said she heard the rumors that Taliban supporters had moved into Bosnia. "I am worried sick," she wrote. After 9/11, ten-year-old Cristina, living near New York City, wrote that she stayed at home alone with her

Unfortunately, some kids' awareness of the world's dark side is a result of feeling its impact more directly.

nine-year-old sister. "I am afraid the hijackers will come and hurt my sister and I. What do I do?"

Many kids seem to appreciate the role strong leadership can play in making the world better. After President Kennedy's assassination in 1963, we heard from many readers. Pamela, age 12, wrote: "On Sunday, I was sick about President Kennedy. He was a young, beloved man. He was a good president . . . I will pray for President Kennedy." In 1993, Melissa, interested in improving life in her Maryland community, wrote: "My parents told me who my congress-woman is. I want to write her a letter, but I don't know anything about her. What can I do?" Andrew, a reader in 1980, wrote that he watched the news, and it seemed that everyone was fighting. He was afraid of war, he said. "I just wish all the leaders of countries could sit down and talk their problems out instead of fighting. Is there anything I can do to help . . . so we can all live together as friends and not have enemies?"

We like to think that kids like Melissa and Andrew, serious and passionate, grow to become leaders themselves, capable and courageous, facing fears to tackle difficult problems. Of course, the problems that resonate deeply with children sometimes lose their urgency as kids mature. But we hope that by encouraging their youthful curiosity, they'll remain interested in world events all their lives. By affirming in our conversations the goodness—the *rightness*—of their wish to be part of the solution, we help kids believe they can make a difference. And we hope that whatever path in life they choose, they will never lose their empathy for all living things across the globe.

THE LETTERS

Dear Highlights,
There are homeless people I always see when My
family drives somewhere. I want to make their lives
better. Please tell me some ways! ☺

—Taylor, 2014

Dear Highlights,
I want to help the homeless, the hungry and others who need help. The problem is I am only thirteen and do not have the money they ask for on television. Is there anything I could do without giving money?

—Kim, 1989

Dear Kim,

We appreciate your desire to help. It's people like you who make our world a better place.

Donating money is only one way to help people. You might also become a volunteer at a local hospital, nursing home, day-care center, or charity dealing with the homeless. You might write an editorial for the school newspaper or give a presentation in class that will help others realize that people are in need of help. Just talking to friends about the homeless and the hungry makes your friends aware of those problems.

If you haven't already done so, we would encourage you to talk to your parents about this. They may have some ideas for how you and other family members can reach out and help those who are homeless. For example, your family might want to find a place of worship or community organization that is working to serve the homeless and then discuss ways to help this organization.

Dear Highlights,
Everywhere I go I see litter.
It seems people just don't
care. I am very careful
about not littering but what
else can I do?
—Sarah, 1985

Dear Highlights,
People are pollution the area I
live in. There is way too much
garbage and not too many people
are doing recycling. Most of
the people don't even care. I go
around picking up garbage, but
I am just one person and there
is a whole lot of pollution. If
someone doesn't do something
there will be no Earth.
—Erin, 1993

Dear Sarah,

One thing you can do is to get others involved, too. Maybe your scout troop, class, or club could make a project to spend a day picking up litter in your neighborhood. If other people see that young people are willing to spend their day picking up litter, they might think twice about throwing their litter around. Another idea is to remind people how bad littering is. You could write a letter to your local newspaper. And why not also write a letter to your school newspaper if you have one? Write to your city council and suggest ways the council could help stop littering. Maybe you think the city needs a strong anti-littering law or maybe there should be more trash cans on the streets. Sarah, one of the things that makes our country work is the involvement of its citizens. If you are concerned about this litter problem, we are sure you will find lots of ways to get involved in trying to improve it.

Dr. Martin Luther King, Jr.

Dr. King believed
In equal rights for all.
Brotherhood for every man
Was his call.

His dream was that man stop living
In the segregated past,
To live in harmony
And be free at last.

—Shiela, age 12, 1978

—Ron, 1990

Dear Highlights,

MY WORLD IS TURNING UPSIDEDOWN!

AHHH! There are TONS of fires. I have a ~~tortoise~~ who lives outside with all the smoke, I'm afraid I'll move to Michigan with my family and would be taken away from my BFF which has already happened, and that scared me, I'm afraid our house will catch fire and don't know how I'd fit all my stuffies, and I have a very tight ^school^ schedule.

PLEASE HELP ME!!!

I HATE 2020!!!

~~2020~~

Worst year of my LIFE 2020

My tummy's twisting & turnin all day!

I've barly been able to sleep for **WEEKS!**

AHHH!

—Heidi, age 10, 2020

Dear Heidi,

We're very sorry that so many worries are weighing on you. Please know that you aren't alone. This year has been a difficult one, especially because we're dealing with so many stressful things at once.

Try to be kind to yourself. What that means is to take good care of your mind and body. Be sure to drink lots of water, eat healthy foods, and get plenty of exercise and rest. To help you sleep better, try going to bed and waking up at the same time each day, avoiding sugar, caffeine, and exciting or scary shows or video games before bed. Try listening to relaxing music before you go to sleep.

You might also find it helpful to talk about how you're feeling with a trusted adult. While adults can't solve all the problems that are happening right now, sometimes just talking about what scares you with someone who cares can help you feel better.

We hope this helps, Heidi. We'll get through this! Please know that you can write to us anytime, and we'll always write back.

Dear Highlights, I want
to raise some money for
some kids in Haiti. I don't
have many ideas. I do
know about freind ship
braclets and earrings & stuff
But I don't have the materi
materials. Do you have any
ideas? (Besides BFF Braclets
+ Earrings + Pictures)

—Morgan, 2013

Dear Morgan,

We're proud of you for wanting to raise money to donate to children in Haiti. What a kind thing to do!

We've enclosed three articles [from *Highlights*] with this letter that we hope will provide some inspiration. One is an article called "Kids at Work," and the other two are part of our "Gallant Kids" feature. We encourage you to get creative and use your imagination. We know you'll come up with some fun ways to raise money.

Here are a few ideas for you. It might help to start by making a list of all your skills and interests. Write down everything you can think of, even if you're not sure how it will help. Then look at your finished list and brainstorm ways to turn those interests into jobs. For example, if you like to cook, maybe you could put together a book of recipes and try selling it to neighbors, friends, and family. If you have a lot of old clothes or toys that you no longer want, you and your parents might consider having a yard sale. You might also ask your parents if there are any chores you can do around the house, such as cleaning or helping out with younger siblings. If your parents say it's OK, you could also ask your neighbors what other kinds of small jobs they need done.

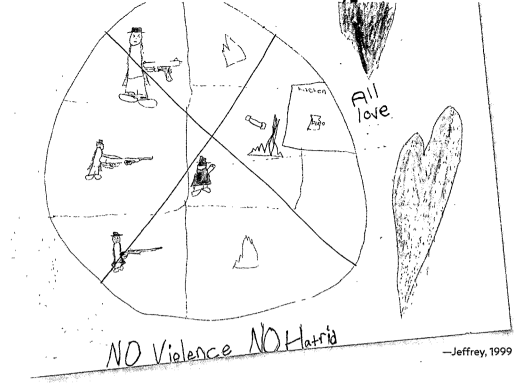

NO Violence NO Hatrid

—Jeffrey, 1999

Dear Jeffrey,

We were impressed to see that the theme of your drawing and its title show that even in the wake of so much tragedy and pain in your community [because of the shooting at Columbine High School], you are able to see what is true, right, and important in life. We can tell that you are a wise and compassionate person. Your message is helpful and healing for everyone, everywhere.

It is people like you and messages like yours that help us all to overcome adversity and tragedy and rise above it. We cannot undo the pain that others inflict, but we can respond to it with determination, as you have, resolving to live our lives with the values that we know to be true and critical. We can refuse to allow others' actions to make us negative, suspicious, unfriendly, and afraid. Living with love toward one another is the only way to live together, and it is love, not guns or bombs or weapons or hate, that has true power. One of its powers is to heal.

No one can force us to harbor hate unless we let them. No one can stop us from interacting with others lovingly. Your drawing and message reminded us of the many wise words of Martin Luther King Jr., when he spoke about nonviolence and love. His message, like yours, was that "Love is the most durable power in the world. This creative force . . . is the most potent instrument available in mankind's quest for peace and security."

Thank you for sharing your drawing and inspiring message with us.

Dear Highlights,

Why should there be problems with inflation? I think they should lower the prices because when my mom and dad try to pay bills they are too much to pay. My friend Sherri doesn't like to buy anything when we go to the mall because she says the prices are too high. What should we do about inflation?

—Lynn, 1980

Dear Lynn,

Inflation is a big problem for everyone. Many things cause inflation, and many people have different opinions about stopping it. We asked two of the country's most respected economists to write an article explaining inflation. We hope this article helps you understand a problem we all share.

—Kaci, age 6, 2015

Dear Kaci,

We're glad you decided to write to us, Kaci. We can tell you are a thoughtful, curious person. That's great!

Our economy is complicated, and people in countries all over the world sell various products to people in other countries. Sometimes different countries specialize in providing various products and services. That might be why you see certain countries' names on products more often than other countries' names.

We hope you will talk to your parents about this. They want to know what's on your mind, and they might be able to help you with this question. Your teacher might also have some helpful ideas.

Dear Editor:

I'm 11 years old. I am a Saudi Arabian and this is my first year in Saudi Arabia. I've been living in America all my life, and I like it. I have a suscription to your magazine and I recieve it every month. I'd like to say it's the best magazine I have ever read, and the best I'll ever read.

As you know, since I'm living in Saudi Arabia, we are in the middle of the Gulf war. I'm really scared, since I've never been through a war befor. I've seen missils flying in the air but thanks to god they always get intercepted.

I want to know, how could anybody do such a heartless thing as the Iraqi leader did? Like killing kids and people, and taking over someones elses home and dosn't want to give it back. I just can't understand it. He has been killing ~~other~~ ~~people just~~ his own people just to save himself. How could anybody be like that. And what makes a person ~~so~~ do such a thing. I just can't understand it.

I hope you understand my feelings. I hate war, and I hope it ends fast, and I hope they kill that heartless Saddam Husain. Please tell me what made him do such things, and how can I keep calm. Thank you!

—Abdul, age 11, 1991

Dear Abdul,

We don't think anyone really knows why Saddam Hussein invaded Kuwait. It's very hard to understand how someone could have done all those terrible things. Some people believe the war was started because Iraq wanted control of the Kuwaiti oil. Other people think that it was started because Saddam Hussein wanted to show how powerful he was. People have different ideas on why the war was started, but probably the only one who knows for sure is Saddam Hussein himself.

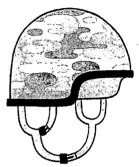

Abdul, we can imagine how scary it must be for you to be in Saudi Arabia. Even now that the war is over, we bet it is still scary. It might help if you try to talk to someone about your fears. One of your parents or a trusted friend might be able to help. Let them know how you are feeling about the war. They might have some suggestions that will keep you calm. Sometimes just sharing your fears with someone else can help you to feel better.

We hope you are safe and healthy, and that this letter helps you. We'll be thinking about you.

Dear Highlights,
Not long ago, Soviets and Americans hooked two rockets together, one from each country. They did this to make friends, yet each country is sending up satellites to spy on each other. They do this to see if each country is planning to attack. If they want to make friends, why are they spying on each other?
                                                              —Richard, 1976

Dear Richard,

We think your question is a very good one, but one which we are not able to answer. It does seem strange, but if our working on the space project with the Soviets can help us live in peace, then it must be worthwhile.

The Horror of War

Oh, the horror of war is very
Bad.
If you live in a free country,
You should be glad.
The people who have seen war,
Want it to cease.
So let's pray that our world will
Be at peace.

—Terry, age 10, 1958

—Vani and Anusha, 2006

Dear Highlights,
I really get disturbed by the awful things that happen in the political and physical world. How can I make the world better without going off to war or running for President?

—Ariel, age 13, 2019

Dear Ariel,

We think your attitude is wonderful. We wish everyone were willing to use their feelings of frustration as motivation to make things better. The world needs more people like you!

It might be helpful to start by making a list of the things on your mind. Writing things down can help us prioritize our thoughts, make worries feel less over-whelming and more manageable, and help us map out a course of action.

Once you've made a list, you can study the items, one by one, and think about what you'd like to focus on and how you might help. If pollution makes you sad, you could help out at local community cleanups, with your parents' permission, or reduce the use of plastics in your life. If you're upset by people who act unkindly, you could start your own kindness campaign, by saying at least ten kind things per day, especially to kids who seem to need it. Or if you'd like to make changes at school, perhaps it's serving in a leadership role—by running for student council or class president, you can inspire others to get involved, too.

One person can start a ripple effect of positive change. There is a famous quote attributed to Margaret Mead, which you might find inspiring: "Never doubt that a small group of thoughtful, committed citizens can change the world; indeed, it's the only thing that ever has."

When you feel sad and over-whelmed by what's going on in the world, it's important to take care of yourself and to reach out to those who love and care about you. When we are healthy and happy ourselves, we are best able to do the work of helping make the world a better place.

Dear Highlights,
What gives government officials the right to wipe out our national parks and wildlife areas just to build superhighways and skyscrapers? What can I do about it?
—Shelton, 1975

Dear Highlights,
I am very concerned about helping to preserve wildlife, so I wrote to a company that was helping with this problem. They told me to learn more about the survival of animals that are becoming extinct. However, I don't see how that could help. How can it help? If you know of anyone who can help me, please let me know. I am very, very serious about this terrible problem.
—Susan, 1972

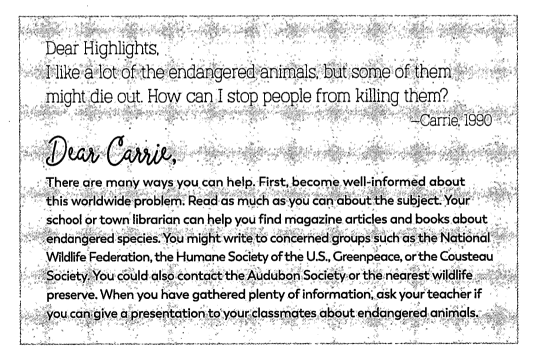

Dear Highlights,
I like a lot of the endangered animals, but some of them might die out. How can I stop people from killing them?
—Carrie, 1990

Dear Carrie,

There are many ways you can help. First, become well-informed about this worldwide problem. Read as much as you can about the subject. Your school or town librarian can help you find magazine articles and books about endangered species. You might write to concerned groups such as the National Wildlife Federation, the Humane Society of the U.S., Greenpeace, or the Cousteau Society. You could also contact the Audubon Society or the nearest wildlife preserve. When you have gathered plenty of information, ask your teacher if you can give a presentation to your classmates about endangered animals.

If I had a magic wand, I would make
  everybody nicer.
I would make the poor have some more
  money;
Make people who are sad, happy;
Make people who are sick, healthy;
Make people who are crying, laugh;
Make the wars stop so there is peace in
the world.
If I had a magic wand, everyone would be
friends and
  No one would be afraid of people who
are different.

—Carl, age 8, 2000

—Ayisha,
age 8, 2015

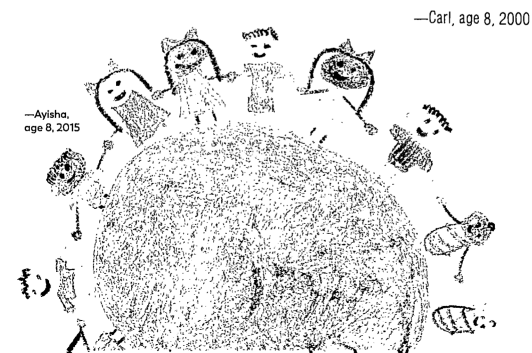

The Brave Seven

It was the best of times, the worst of times,
that's how a classic started,
like people who were once so happy,
now are broken-hearted.
They're the loved ones of brave people,
who now are sadly gone,
their once happily bright faces,
now are grimly drawn.
A teacher rode the shuttle,
the first teacher into space,
for that she eagerly waited,
with a smile upon her face.
Six astronauts accompanied her,
but little did they know
that along with her, they'd lose their lives,
and the things that they love so.
So now let's take a moment,
to think of those brave seven,
who, on the wings of the Challenger,
Have soared their way to heaven.

—Spencer, age 11, 1986

—Garrett, 2003

Dear Highlights,

I need help! my family does not like Donald Trump. Why I need Help is Because I am afraid that my family is splitting up! I am super emotional. I don't know what to do because my mom said if Donald starts rounding people up she is moving to CANADA and my dad might stay in USA! PLEASE HELP.

Thank you for reading,
your fan,

I LOVE HIGHLIGHT!

—Alex, age 10, 2016

Dear Alex,

We've heard from other kids who have questions or concerns about the election and its results, so it may help you feel better to know that you're not alone.

Sometime when things are quiet and your parents aren't busy with other things, you might say you would like to talk with them about something that has been bothering you. Then you can go on to explain how you feel when you hear them talk about President-elect Trump or moving out of the country. We believe they will want to know how upset you are when you hear such things.

Sometimes when people get upset, they say things they don't mean. We've all done it because we're all human and our emotions get the best of us occasionally. It can help to give people time and space when they're upset. Then, if you'd like, you might talk about the situation later on when they're feeling calmer. If your parents start talking about the election results, you might quietly leave the room and do something you enjoy, such as reading, working on an art project, writing in a journal, or listening to music.

Dear Highlights,
Two boys walked into the class on November 22, 1963, saying someone killed President Kennedy. When I heard that I almost cried, but when I got home I listened to the radio and it was true. I bet in fifty years I will still remember the day when President Kennedy was shot.

—James, age 8, 1964

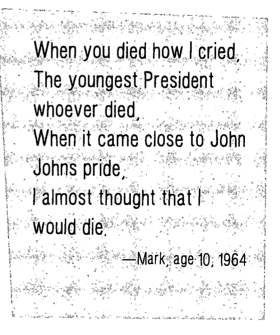

When you died how I cried,
The youngest President whoever died,
When it came close to John John's pride,
I almost thought that I would die.

—Mark, age 10, 1964

Now it's 76,
Time to celebrate.
Time to eat the candy,
Time to eat the cake.
We're 200 year old now,
We're happy and having fun.
We've signed the Declaration of
Independence
and Constitution
We hope this year is better
Then all the ones before
Then 1973
and 1974

　　　—Annette, age 9, 1976

Dear Highlights,

I'm scared for the turnout of the presidential election. My friends talk about it all the time, and it really makes me uncomfortable. What should I do?

—Sydney, 2016

Dear Sydney,

We're sorry this is troubling you, Sydney. Although it's good that your friends have been talking about the election, we can see why you might like to talk and hear about something else. We've heard from other kids as well as adults who feel the same way.

By the time you receive this letter, the election will be over, and we will know who our new president will be in January. Gradually, the discussions about the campaign and election will calm down, and we can turn our attention to other things.

Your parents or another trusted adult might be able to offer you tips on politely changing the subject when your friends are talking about something that troubles you.

Dear Highlights,
I live in New York City. There are some neighborhoods that were hit pretty badly by Hurricane Sandy. My neighborhood is fine, but I still want to help in any way I can. I am eleven years old. Do you have any suggestions on how a kid my age can help?

—Annika, age 11, 2012

Dear Annika,

In addition to donating money, food, water, and clothing, there may be some hands-on work, such as cleanup, that you and your family can do together. You and your parents might ask others in your neighborhood to pitch in, too. If you attend a place of worship, a leader there may already be organizing some kind of relief effort in which you and your family could participate.

The schools in the disaster area may need to be restocked with books and other supplies, or maybe students in your own school need help. Your school or you and your classmates could focus fundraising efforts in that way. Your teacher or guidance counselor will know if this is a possibility at your school or in your community.

The Red Cross, well-known for its help with disaster relief, has set up an area on its website that gives information on how elementary-school kids can start their own Red Cross club and help out. With your parent's permission, you can go to it and get the information you need.

The coming months will be an especially challenging time for the people affected by the hurricane. The courage, kindness, and compassion of the people who are helping are rays of hope that will give strength and encouragement in the months ahead. We're proud of you for wanting to do your part to make things better, Annika.

Now We See a Ray of Hope

A Poem for the Victims of Hurricane Katrina

Now we see a ray of hope
Shining through the sky
Piercing through the clouds of
death, in this tragic time.
A dove of peace soars overhead,
and bestows upon this town,
A feeling to smile, a feeling to grin
A feeling not to frown.
Let those who are obsessed
by death be obsessed by Joy.
And let us help the children, all
the little girls and boys.
Wash away the filth of sadness,
the dirt of cruelty and sin
And help us all to look inside;
to feel the Joy within.

—Whitney, age 10, 2005

—Sasha, 2006

I never knew
that it would
happen to us
until one day
the bomb went up.
I hoped and prayed
in a very special
way that no more
family members would
disappear on that day

—Stephanie, 1995

Dear Ms. Fielder and Students,*

We can't imagine the sadness and fear that all of you experienced over the bombing of the federal building [in Oklahoma City]. Although we experienced the disaster at a distance, we, too, mourn for those who died. Children in particular can have a very difficult time putting their fears to rest. You were wise to have your students express their feelings about the bombing. Thank you for sending their poems to Highlights. We are pleased that they shared them with us. Best wishes to you and all your students from all of us at Highlights.

*A third-grade teacher from Oklahoma City, whose school was located four miles from the federal building bombing in 1995, shared her students' poems with Highlights. Ms. Fielder wrote that she and her class heard the bombing and felt the windows shake. She asked her students to write about how they felt several days after the event, and hoped that the poems would "give children nationwide an understanding of this disaster from a child's point of view."

Dear Highlights,
A tragedy just happened in my neighborhood! The Boston Marathon was bombed and I live very near! It's very hectic and everyone keeps calling us to see if we are ok. I'm getting soooooooooooooo nervous!! I don't know what to do. If you have any advice I would REALLY appreciate it.

—Celeste, 2013

Dear Celeste,

We hope you'll discuss your feelings with a parent or another trusted adult. Talking things over with someone who cares about you can ease your mind. And remember your parents are there for you for extra hugs and encouragement.

We understand that people calling to see if you and your family are OK can add to the feeling of chaos now. They're checking on you out of love and concern, which is a good thing. As time passes, the phone calls will lessen, and your family's routine can return to normal.

It may help you to remember that your parents, teachers, principals, and other people in your community, including police officers and firefighters, are doing everything they can to be sure that you and others are safe every day. Knowing that they're doing their jobs may give you a sense of peace.

Sticking to your regular routine may help you feel that things are getting back to normal. Going to school, working hard on your homework, eating healthy foods and exercising, getting enough rest, and spending time with your family and friends can help focus on positive things. When you think about it, a wonderful way for us to honor the victims of the tragedy is to remain strong and enjoy everyday life. It's not that we're forgetting about what happened—we're realizing what a precious gift life is and that it should be lived and enjoyed to its fullest every single day.

To Live Free Today

I've been to New York City,
What happened there's a pity,
Lots of people are gone,
Smoke was still there by dawn,
Lets hope soon its clear,
And that it never happens here,
Our young men may go to war,
And our taxes may be more,
But that's the price you pay,
To live free today.

AMERICA
THE
BEAUTIFUL

—Rebecca, 2001

Dear Rebecca,

We can tell by your poem that you are experiencing great sadness about the tragic events of September 11. Everyone here at Highlights feels sad, too. It is the natural way to feel about events such as this.

It's important to remember that many people love you and are looking after you. Government leaders and others in the U.S. and around the world are working hard to keep you safe, too.

Writing a poem is an excellent way to express your feelings. We hope you will continue to share your feelings with those you trust, perhaps your parents, a close relative, a teacher, a school counselor, or a clergyperson. It truly helps when someone who cares about us listens while we share our feelings and talk about our thoughts.

There are other things you might do to deal with your sadness. You might make more illustrated poems, write in a journal, help your parents hang a flag in front of your home, or make memorial ribbons for people to wear. Many people find it helpful to attend religious or memorial services for all the families touched by this tragedy. Even making an extra effort to be kind and loving to your family, friends, and neighbors can make you feel a little less sad.

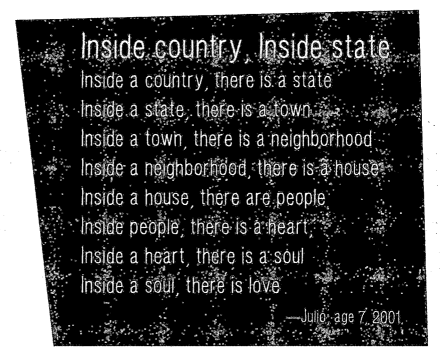

Inside country, Inside state

Inside a country, there is a state
Inside a state, there is a town
Inside a town, there is a neighborhood
Inside a neighborhood, there is a house
Inside a house, there are people
Inside people, there is a heart
Inside a heart, there is a soul
Inside a soul, there is love

—Julio, age 7, 2001

The Dust of September

The dust of September
The dust, the smoke, the clouds
From the dust of September.
The sadness, the sorrow, the darkness
From the dust of September.
The pretty sites are gone, the love, the death
From the dust of September.
The families, the lives taken away
From the dust of September.
Our country is sad, but our country still stands
In the dust of September.
Our flag still waves,
Through the dust of September.
We will never break, we will stand together
Through the dust of September

—Vanessa, 2001

United We Stand

United we stand, you apart, can't break us comes for real democracy LADY from the heart! Liberty's torch shows peace for all races; black, white, for all different faces. The Liberty Bell rings with pride, so may all free our country, Your people be of lies. the feathered angel like a above. Stars and stripes are forever, can anyone take us over? Never! This nation is very free of slaves, that is why the we are, and the land of the free, and the brave. home of

—Lauren, age 8, 2001

—Daniel, 2001

Billy

Billy was silly at times
Other times he was helpful
When a tragedy struck
He would always help
His poor dear old mother
But when this tragedy struck us by surprise
Billy was nowhere in sight
We thought and we thought
We then remembered
Billy was at work
He worked in the first Twin Tower

We waited and waited
Prayed and we prayed
Day by day
Night by night
Then came a call, we did not want to hear
They found Billy
Under the rubble, caused by bin Laden
But the bad thing was
they found him dead.

In loving memory of my cousin 1956–2001

—Brandon, age 11, 2002

The Statue of Liberty

—Kelsey, age 8, 2002

WORLD—TRADE— CENTER

—Kayla, 2001

Letters About

Biases & Exclusion

KIDS ARE DEEPLY AFFECTED BY STEREOTYPES AND unjustified negative attitudes about those who are "different," whether they are victims, offenders, or bystanders. Although it was once commonly believed that young kids don't see skin color, we now know that kids notice differences in people's physical traits, such as skin color, even before age 2 or 3. Around the same age, kids recognize differences in gender. Very soon thereafter, they can internalize all the biases they pick up from parents, grandparents, teachers, peers, books, movies, and other media. By the time kids outgrow *Highlights*, around age 12, many of their beliefs about people have started to gel. Knowing this, we're reminded that it's never too soon to talk to kids about differences.

It's sad but true: Kids (and adults) can be insensitive and even, at times, cruel. Kids who do not have a broad, culturally diverse social network or who have not been privy to enlightening conversations about inclusion and equity sometimes ask questions or seek information in ways that can be hurtful. They may unfairly place the responsibility of educating themselves about differences on the people they want to understand, instead of accepting the responsibility themselves. In 1999, Nabila, an eleven-year-old Muslim, wrote: "I get asked over and over again why do I wear a hijab. All the questioning each day gets me mad. What should I do?"

Some kids knowingly inflict pain with name-calling that deeply wounds. They bully others and deny their victims friendship or any sense of belonging.

By the time kids outgrow *Highlights*, around age 12, many of their beliefs about people have started to gel. Knowing this, we're reminded that it's never too soon to talk to kids about differences.

Over the years, these are the most common acts of racism kids have shared with us. In 1993, Trinity wrote, "I go to a White school. Sometimes they make fun of my color. What should I do?" A reader named Kimi in 2008 wrote to say that she gets teased because she is part Blackfoot Indian. "I like being Indian," she said, "but it hurts my feelings a lot. Can you help?" In 2010, we received an email from a child who revealed a peer conversation. "At camp, a boy said he hated Chinese people, which my friend is," the reader wrote.

"Then he said Chinese people stink. Everyone in the back of the bus laughed and smirked."

Similarly, we've heard from kids who are teased, bullied, or ostracized because of differences in religious beliefs. Those who practice a faith outside of their community's dominant culture are most at risk, but prejudice, ironically, doesn't discriminate; we've received letters about religious intolerance from kids of many different faiths.

We also hear from kids who suffer because they don't meet cultural expectations related to gender identity, sexuality, and stereotypical gender roles. In 1971, Tammy wrote: "I have a problem. I hate to play with the girls, but I love to play with the boys. I only play jump rope when I have to. I love to play basketball, baseball, kickball, tetherball, and other boys' games." In 1989, Danny wrote to us about his newfound love of knitting. "I tried knitting and got the hang of it, but my mom thinks it's for girls only. I seem to like this knitting." One might expect that over time society would grow less rigid about cultural "norms" related to gender and kids' interests. However, 15 years later, Sean sent a similar letter: "I love sewing so much!!!!! But here I'm aka the Sewing Sissy. I'm often mocked at because I like a girl thing." Throughout the years and still today, we have heard from girls who worry that their female gender will be a barrier to achieving their career goals.

We sometimes receive letters from kids questioning their gender identity. In 2020, Addison wrote, "So lately, I've been thinking more about my pronouns and gender identity. Currently I'm a girl, but I don't exactly feel like a whole girl, if you know what I mean. So, I've been a little confused. Am I non-binary, or a demigirl, or genderfluid, or am I just psyching myself out?" From time to time, children reach out to talk about the prejudice they encounter for having LGBTQ parents.

People with disabilities are also subjected to thoughtless and hurtful comments from peers. Over the years, children with various disabilities have written to share their wish to be seen as people with strengths. In 2009, one child who uses a wheelchair put it this way: "People point and laugh and stare," he said. "But I am smart, and can write poetry, but everyone focuses on my disability. Do you have any tips for me to keep people focused on the boy in the chair?" Often unable to advocate for themselves, these kids are sometimes supported by friends and siblings who ask for advice on their behalf. In 1983, Jodi wrote in support of her brother, who was called names and taunted for needing special resources in school. Almost every letter and email on this subject reinforces the need to help able-bodied kids better empathize with those who live with disabilities, unlearn what is hurtful behavior, and show appropriate ways to be supportive.

Our replies to all letters about biases and exclusion have evolved over the years, as our understanding of these issues has deepened. This is particularly true of our replies to kids confronting racism. As we look back at decades-old correspondence, we see that although our responses were always intended to be supportive, helpful, and reflective of the best thinking in child psychology and education at the time, we now know better. After the Black Lives Matter movement more fully captured the attention of our nation in 2020, we very purposely reviewed how we have talked to kids who wrote to us about being mistreated or disrespected because of race. Sometimes we failed to name the behavior our readers were writing about, which was racism. We tried to acknowledge it and condemn it by talking about celebrating our differences and acknowledging all the many ways we are alike. But today, we understand better the importance of helping kids recognize prejudice of all kinds so they can challenge it when they see or experience it.

As we sifted through our archives of letters, it was dispiriting to see how many letters we received from kids who sensed they were feared, ridiculed, pushed away, or dismissed because of perceived differences. But we were heartened to also find letters similar to the one from eleven-year-old Rhiannon, who wrote in 2012: "I've been learning about segregation and I want to know. Why are people with dark skin treated differently? Even now? Why is it such a big deal? its just a skin tone."

While it's true that it's never too soon to talk to kids about differences, it's also never too late. The decade between toddlerhood and the teenage years—the *Highlights* window—is a critically important time for encouraging kids to recognize and challenge stereotypes and biases. But that doesn't mean it's easy. Many adults find it awkward to talk with their children about other people's differences, even though it is a subject that is often on kids' minds. Listening to children tell their own stories about experiencing and observing discriminatory talk and behaviors can open the door to the honest, straightforward conversations kids want and need. These discussions foster in them an appreciation for diversity, inclusion, kindness, and empathy.

Today, we understand better the importance of helping kids recognize prejudice of all kinds so they can challenge it when they see it or experience it.

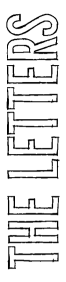

Dear Highlights,
Being twelve, I just hit puberty. I'm starting to get feelings for people. The problem is, I have a crush on a girl in my class, but I'm also a girl. Only few people know I'm bi. But I want to tell her, but it's so stressful, what if she doesn't want to be my friend afterwards? I'm scared I'll be judged by my fellow classmates. My teacher and my mom already know. Please help!

—Mackenzie, age 12, 2019

Dear Mackenzie,

It's good that you've talked to your mom and your teacher. We encourage you to continue to confide in them whenever you have questions or just want to talk.

It's difficult to say what would happen if you told your classmate you have special feelings for her. Because you're concerned that it might affect your friendship, it might be a good idea to wait. It's true that sometimes people act differently after learning that someone has a crush on them. Try to remember that you'll have plenty of time later in life to have romantic relationships. Now is a good time to form meaningful friendships and participate in activities you enjoy.

It's up to you to decide what personal details you want to share with your classmates. Some people may be judgmental, and others may be accepting. What's important is that you do what makes you feel most comfortable at a time that feels right for you. Try not to feel pressured to share anything you're not quite ready to share. Telling yourself that there's no rush may relieve some of the stress you've been feeling.

Dear Highlights,

My father is being racist and I told him to stop. Then he talks about the Declaration of Independence and says, "I have the right of free speech." I know that my dad is right, but he should at least consider my feelings. Pretty please help—I have done everything I could from counselor to asking my dad to pretty please stop.

—Anonymous, 2013

Dear Friend,

Thank you for your message. We're sorry that your dad's behavior has been bothering you. We think it was smart to share your feelings with your dad and to talk with a counselor. We can see how you might feel angry or upset if nothing has worked.

Although we've never met your dad, we're sure that he loves you very much, even when he disagrees with you. It might help to remember that although you cannot control what other people say or think, you can control how you react to their words. No one is perfect and, unfortunately, nearly everyone has made an unfair judgment or chosen to believe a negative stereotype at one time or another. It's difficult to know why this happens. Often, people's opinions are influenced by experiences they had when they were younger, or by the thoughts and perspectives of their parents, friends, or role models.

Ultimately, you can't force your dad to take your perspective. You can, however, use your own words and actions to treat people of all races equally. Over time, it's possible that your dad may choose to change his perspective.

Your other relatives may have good advice, too. We hope you'll continue to ask for suggestions anytime you're worried or unhappy.

Dear Highlights,

I am a girl and I am the biggest baseball fan ever! Whenever I wore baseball clothes out in public or to a game, I get called a boy. How do I tell them that im not,

—Jocelyn, age 11, 2015

Dear Highlights,
I want to play football, but my mom said no, and my dad said I might not be able to take the hits since I'm a girl. I really want to play. Any advice?

—Anonymous, 2015

Dear Jocelyn,

We're sorry people keep confusing you for a boy when you're dressed in your baseball clothes. We're sure that is frustrating. The good news is your self-worth and identity do not have to depend on what other people say about you. You are free to dress in baseball clothes. If people think you're a boy, try not to let it get to you.

Depending on the situation, you could either ignore it when people call you a boy, or you could politely correct them, maybe laughing it off so they don't feel bad. For example, you could laugh kindly and say, "Oh, actually I'm a girl. It's a common mistake!" If you can act lighthearted about the situation, then it won't seem as though you are upset.

We hope this helps. Your parents may have some advice for you as well.

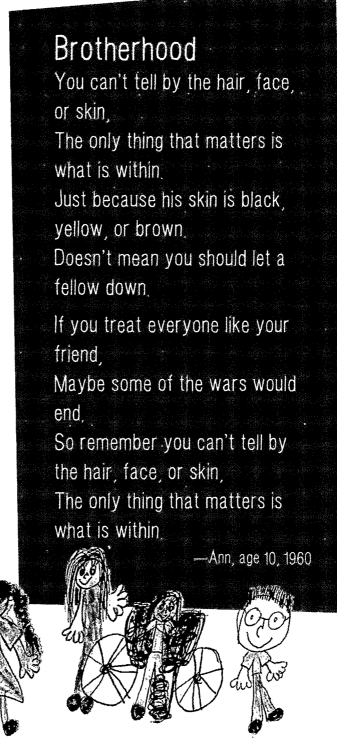

Brotherhood

You can't tell by the hair, face,
or skin,
The only thing that matters is
what is within.
Just because his skin is black,
yellow, or brown.
Doesn't mean you should let a
fellow down.

If you treat everyone like your
friend,
Maybe some of the wars would
end.
So remember you can't tell by
the hair, face, or skin,
The only thing that matters is
what is within.

—Ann, age 10, 1960

—Madeleine, age 7, 2004

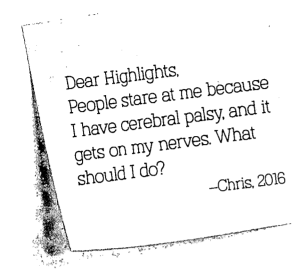

Dear Highlights,
People stare at me because I have cerebral palsy, and it gets on my nerves. What should I do?

—Chris, 2016

Dear Highlights,
I have Cerebral Palsy (I am in a wheel chair) so that makes me lean a lot and I can't help it. People keep asking me to "correct my posture" meaning to sit up and it gets on my nerves. I've asked them politely to stop telling me (many times) but they keep doing it. HELP!!!!

—Anonymous, 2013

Dear Friend,

We can understand how it would be frustrating that people keep trying to correct your posture. We're sorry this is happening, but we're proud of you for speaking up about your cerebral palsy. Although the people telling you to sit up may not understand your situation, we're sure that other kids with cerebral palsy would share your frustration with these comments!

These people may not realize how much their comments upset you. If you see them regularly (if they're friends or relatives) you might share your feelings in one-on-one conversations. You could say something such as, "I feel a little frustrated when you bring up my posture, which I can't really change." Try to choose a time when you're getting along and speak in a calm tone. If they understand your point of view, they may be more likely to avoid saying things like this in the future.

We hope you'll ask your parents for advice, too. They would want to know about anything that's on your mind, and we believe they would be happy to offer their ideas and support.

I came from TURKEY. And I'm a new student in my class. my friends make fun of me. and they tell me that I'm a turkey. what I can do to stop them telling me turkey.

—Orhan, 1993

Dear Orhan,

Some kids tease others for the silliest reasons. Sometimes they do it for attention. If you show these kids that it doesn't bother you when they call you a turkey, they'll probably get bored and stop saying it. The next time someone teases you, pretend not to listen. Concentrate on whatever you're doing or just walk away.

Things must be very different for you, now that you're living in the United States. We'll bet some of your classmates would be interested to know what life is like in Turkey. Perhaps you could show them some examples of things you do here and how they're done in your native country. Maybe you could even bring in some photographs to show them.

We hope this is helpful. All of us wish you the best.

Dear Highlights,

My &r two friends and I are Unatarian wich believe that all beliefs are right. A girl isn't aloud to play with us Unatarians becau her mom didn't like our beliefs. But we play the same stuf she does and I don't want to kick her out. What should I do?

—Nicole, age 10, 2000

Dear Nicole,

We're sorry you're having this problem. Maybe you have noticed that people's beliefs vary a great deal. This doesn't mean that one belief is wrong and another is right. Everyone has a right to his or her own beliefs. We're sure you understand that your friend's mother's feelings about your beliefs represent her opinion; they do not mean that there is anything wrong with your religion.

We hope you will talk with your parents about your concern. They may have some good suggestions for you.

In the meantime, you can be supportive and friendly to this girl and let her know that you understand the problem.

Dear Highlights,
A boy in my class always gets teased because of his color. I don't like it. What should I do?

—Kim, 1981

Dear Kim,

You must be very sensitive and kind to be worried about the boy in your class. We don't think you can control what others say about him. However, you can be friends with him. He'll probably be happy to know that he can count on you not to tease him.

Keep the Dream

Peace is like a rolling wave
   that has not yet reached the shore,
Growing bigger every day as people accept
it more.

Will it become a tidal wave
   and bring peace to all our land?
It's up to us to keep the dream
   and give it a helping hand.

Accepting others as they are
   and not what you wish them to be,
Stop racism, hate, and violence against
each other—
   this is the key.

It's up to us to choose its fate,
Stop all crime, racism, and hate
Let peace roll gently to the shore
   and flood our land forevermore.

—Michael, age 11, 1995

—Oviya, age 9, 2015

It's hard being Jewish

I am Jewish. I am the only Jewish girl in 5th grade. There is a boy too. I feel so left out. It's hard to convince my friends I am just like them but a different religion. What should I do?

—Naomi, 1982

Dear Highlights,
This year I'm going to a new school. It's a public school and I'm Jewish. I'm a little nervous.

—Aviva, age 8, 2019

Dear Aviva,

We receive many letters from kids who have back-to-school jitters, especially when they're going to a new school.

It's likely that there will be kids of all different religions at your new school. These students will probably be curious and eager to learn more about your religious traditions. This is a great chance for you to learn more about other faith traditions, too. If anyone makes unkind remarks about your religion, try your best to talk it out with them. If you feel threatened by the things they say, be sure to tell your parents and a teacher or school counselor about it. Every student has the right to feel safe and comfortable at school.

Dear Highlights,

Hi I may be a little told old for this but u guys have helped me in the past. I'm gay and I don't know how to explain it to my friends and or classmates. A lot of people just don't get it and I'm constantly hearing jokes and other stuff about sexuality. Do you have any tips to coming out to them? Anything would help. Thank you.

—Lily, 2011

Dear Lily,

It might help to know you're not alone. We hear from other kids who have similar problems.

The way you handle telling your friends and classmates that you're gay should be in a way that feels most natural for you. There's probably no need to make a big announcement about it. You might tell a couple of your closest friends first, and you could even start by saying, "This is kind of hard for me to talk about, but since you're my good friends, I'd like you to know." Once you have the support of your friends, it might be easier to bring it up in other situations when it seems appropriate.

It's true that people make a lot of jokes about sexuality in general. Young people especially joke about sex because they're trying to figure out something they don't know much about, and they're trying to make themselves feel more comfortable with the whole idea. Try to remember that these jokes are often a sign of immaturity and aren't worth paying attention to.

It would be a good idea to speak to a school guidance counselor about your concerns. He or she has probably counseled other kids in similar situations and might have helpful thoughts or suggestions. Writing in a journal is also a good way to let go of some worries and figure out how to express what's on your mind.

If you feel comfortable doing so, we hope you'll talk to your parents about this. Your parents love you and want to know what you're going through, and they might have some good ideas.

Dear Highlights,
i am a extreme republican and other kids bully me about it saying
i'm a racist but im not. kids are really bullying me help!

—Carter, age 13, 2020

Dear Carter,

Thank you for your letter. We can understand how frustrating it must be to be accused of things that are not true.

You might start by thinking about what might be causing the other kids to say this. When you say you're an "extreme Republican," what does that mean to you, and what might that mean to others? Rather than calling yourself by a label that can be interpreted differently by different people, perhaps you can state your views in more specific ways, such as "I believe that . . ." and "I feel that . . ." That way, other kids might be less likely to misunderstand what you mean. When you're having conversations, remember to keep your voice calm as you speak and to listen closely when others are speaking. By sharing our own views and trying to understand the views of others, we can come to understand each other better.

And, in many cases, actions speak more powerfully than words. If kids see you consistently behaving in anti-racist ways, they may stop accusing you of being racist. Some ways you can do this are by getting to know and becoming friends with kids of different races who will bring different perspectives to your conversations; listening closely to others and trying to understand their opinions; sticking up for kids who are teased because of their race; speaking up when others make racist jokes; reading books by a diverse range of authors about people of different races, including civil-rights heroes; and trying to understand other people's perspectives through conversations. The more we all listen and learn, the better we'll start to understand each other and be able to recognize and fight racism together.

If these kids continue to bully you, it might be best to try to avoid them. It might also be helpful to talk to your parents about this. They love you very much and want to know how you're feeling.

People look different.
Their clothes, their skin and hair.
But when people start Judging,
it makes things Just unfair.

—Lucy, age 11, 2020

Dear Highlights,

So... this could be a long one and I'm just writing this as everything kinda spills out.

I'm sure that everyone is aware about the murder of George Floyd at the hands of four police officers in Minneapolis and the protests it has sparked, as well as once again exposing the systemic racism in this country.

I am someone with a severe anxiety disorder, so it has been hard for me to look at anything regarding the issue. But I am a straight, white teenage girl with a platform that needs to speak up. I feel like I'm being selfish and taking advantage of my white privilege when I start to feel panicked, but I feel like I'm not doing enough with I'm trying to raise awareness. I've sent my parents resources to donate to, but I don't know if they're going to. I've also signed a petition for all four officers involved to be charged with first-degree murder.

I've also thought about joining protests, but I live in West Virginia (a predominantly red state). Plus, we are currently in the middle of a pandemic that's making me on edge as it is, and my mother has Type II diabetes, so I'm afraid that if I contract the coronavirus, I might put her at risk. Not to mention, even before the pandemic, I was already nervous around crowds.

Thank you for your time. I hope all of you stay safe in this frightening time.

—Anonymous, 2020

Dear Friend,

Thank you for your message. We're glad you felt comfortable sharing your feelings about the murder of George Floyd, which are compounded by the worry related to the ongoing pandemic and your own severe anxiety disorder. We are big believers that talking through confusing thoughts and emotions with people who care about us helps us understand our feelings and manage them better.

We can tell from your message that you are a caring and compassionate person—someone who is mindful of the needs of others and wants to help contribute to their well-being. We commend you for recognizing the privileges you have that are denied to many others and for wanting to take action to promote true justice and equality. Please know that all of us here at Highlights are also heartbroken, angered, and distressed about Mr. Floyd's murder and, like you, are struggling to know how to effectively and compassionately respond. You are not alone in this.

You say that you don't think you are doing enough with trying to raise awareness. When there's so much work to be done, our individual actions can feel like a drop in the bucket. It can be easy to get discouraged and overwhelmed, even to the point of paralyzing ourselves. Yet that helps no one.

Here is the thing: Positive action, on any level, is still positive action. Setting your intention to work on behalf of marginalized members of our society is a good first step. Following it up with actions such as signing petitions and making donations to worthy organizations that fight injustice are good ways to support that intention. No act is too small to be significant. Resist the thinking that there's not much you can do to make a difference simply because you don't see the results of your efforts. Petitions can help raise awareness of an issue. A letter you send, even unanswered, may stir compassion and plant a seed of new ways of thinking for someone else—but you may never know it. Find the work that's meaningful to you—work that allows you to use your own talents, skills, and personality traits. That might be writing letters, as we see you do so well. Maybe that work is writing poetry, fundraising,

Continued

241

or doing something else. Your actions don't have to mirror the actions of others. Do your work, trusting that doing so is both its own reward and is making a difference. You are sending out ripples of justice. It will take a lot of ripples, from many people, to wear down hardened, unjust ways. But keep the ripples flowing.

And remember, it's not just the overt actions we take but it's also (and especially) the way we live our lives, the conversations we have, and the behaviors we model that can have profound effects.

If you find yourself starting to feel guilty for not doing more, try to remember that you can't do everything at once. Choose one specific, doable task. It can be something you share with others or something you do for yourself, such as researching the issues that concern you or getting out your emotions and confusion in a journal. Remind yourself that you are focusing on one step to take now—not on everything that needs to be done.

We hope you'll show compassion for yourself as you work for justice. You didn't make a choice to feel panicked, nor is that something you want to feel. In fact, anxiety likely makes many things more difficult for you. Self-compassion is often considered to be a necessary precursor to compassion for others. If you can empathize with your own challenges and emotions, you can better empathize and understand those of others.

Having compassion for everyone includes you. We think you are wise and compassionate to choose to stay safe for your mom's sake—and for your own and others' as well; if you were to catch the virus, you could unwittingly pass it along to not only your mom but to many others, too. And since people of color are being disproportionately hurt by the virus, giving the virus opportunities to spread would be counter to the results that you want.

To learn more ways to dismantle white privilege and combat racism, talk with your parents about other actions you might take, individually and as a family. Perhaps your parents know of other resources in your area that might help you educate yourself, study problems of injustice and inequality, understand others' perspectives and experiences, and take additional steps to make just choices and decisions. As poet and civil rights activist Maya Angelou said, "When you know better, you do better."

We hope these thoughts are helpful. Know that we are in this with you, that we share your struggles, and that we also share your determination to make ongoing positive change. We hope you will write to us again and let us know how you are doing.

Dear Highlights,
I have a special kind of family, where I don't have a mom and dad, I have two dads. I get teased at school because of it. What should I do?

—Alana, 2017

Dear Alana,

It's good to ask for help when you're not sure what to do.

We're sorry that people have been teasing you. Sometimes it's hard to understand why people act the way they do. They may not yet realize that every family is special and wonderful. There are families, like yours, with two dads; there are families with two moms; and there are families with a mom and a dad or with just one parent. There are families with foster parents, adoptive parents, grandparents, or a stepmom or stepdad. The makeup of a family really doesn't matter—what's important is that the family members love and support one another.

With that in mind, you may want to tell yourself that the people who are making fun of you don't really know you and your family very well. If they did, they would see that your family is one that is full of love.

We suggest that you do your best to ignore any comments about your family. If the teasers know their behavior bothers you, they are more likely to continue making the remarks. When possible, avoid being alone around these people; they may be less likely to tease you when you're with others. Continue to spend time with your friends, get involved in activities, and focus on the things that make you happy. Doing this will help make it easier to ignore any teasing.

We hope you will talk to your dads about the things on your mind. They love you and want to know what's going on in your life, and they may have some thoughts that will help. You can also reach out to other trusted adults, such as a teacher or school counselor, who can offer their guidance and support.

August 23, 2006

Dear Higlights,
I have a brother with autism and he cant talk so he does Sign Languge and people make fun of him and i tell them to leave him alone be cause he gets upset when they do that. What should I do?

yours truly

P.S. I started a club called kids with mental disibilities (kwmd). is that a good thing to try to teach my neiborhood about this or not?

—Michelle, 2006

Dear Michelle,

You sound like a kind, thoughtful, and supportive sister, and we're proud to have you as a reader! We think it's wonderful that you stick up for your brother when other kids tease him, and we think it's great that you've started a club to help others understand autism.

We think kids tease others more often when they notice that somebody is different but don't understand why that person is different. By teaching those around you more about autism, you may help them to understand it better and, as a result, they may tease your brother less. They may also become interested in learning some sign language so that they could communicate with your brother.

When you talk to kids who have teased your brother, you might try talking to just one kid at a time. People tend to be kinder, more understanding, and more open-minded when they're not in a group. If you let them know in a calm voice how the teasing makes you and your brother feel, they may be less likely to tease him again, even when they're with a group.

You might also talk to your parents and your brother's doctor about your efforts to teach others about autism. They will probably be glad to know that you're taking an active role in supporting your brother, and they may have helpful suggestions for you and your club.

this is my teacher

this is me doing ballet well I am a boy and it might seem a bit silly but I Like it even though other kids make fun of me!

—Anonymous, 2008

Dear Highlights,

In Music class, my + music teacher only sang christmas songs and I am jewish. My other friends and I who were jewish were upset about it. Then he sang all the other christian holidays, and were jewish. What should we do?

—Sam, age 10, 2001

Dear Sam,

We know that at holiday times (and especially at Christmas time) the whole school may seem to be focused on a celebration that has very little to do with you. We think an acknowledgement of your beliefs is what you are hoping for. It doesn't seem from your letter that you would like to stop your teacher from singing Christmas songs, just that you would like your teacher to add songs that celebrate other beliefs, too.

We suggest you talk to your music teacher about how you feel. He may not realize that this is bothering you. It is also possible that your teacher simply doesn't know any Hanukkah songs. If this is the case, you might want to ask your rabbi, cantor, or another person knowledgeable in Jewish songs and religious practices if he or she can help you find sheet music and words for "I Have a Little Dreidel" or other common songs.

You might also talk to your parents about how you feel. They may have some other suggestions for you.

We're glad to hear you would like to celebrate your religious culture with your classmates. There may be other children in your school who have a religion other than Judaism or Christianity, and by stepping forward and asking your teacher to acknowledge your beliefs, you may give these other students the courage to do the same for their beliefs.

—Malia, age 11, 2005

Every Child of Every Land

Let every child of every land
Join hands in this glad game,
For, though our speech may different
be,
Our laughter is the same.
For, though our speech may different
be,
The same sun shines on all,
And loves to see all children glad
That live on this green ball.

—Cathy, age 10, 1953

Dear Highlights,

People make fun of me because I'm Chinese/Japanese. They squint their eyes to mock me and always say "Why are you closing your eyes?" in pictures. People say I'm ugly. Sometimes I feel like I could be a different nationality. What do I do?

–Kiara, 2016

Dear Kiara,

We're so sorry to hear that people are making these ridiculous comments. We hear from many kids who get teased, so you are not alone. We hope you understand that when people make comments like this, it reflects poorly only on those people —not on you! Please try not to let their comments affect the way you feel about yourself. You are a unique and precious person, and the fact that we're all different is a big part of what makes the world interesting and beautiful.

When readers write to us about teasing and bullying, we often suggest that the best response is to completely ignore the comments. Usually teasers are trying to get a reaction, and the more you react, the more satisfying it is to them. However, if it seems appropriate, you could respond to a comment by saying, "You know, that's disrespectful, and I'd appreciate it if you didn't talk like that." While the teasers might not change their behavior immediately, they may think about what you said.

It's important to talk to your parents about the way you're feeling. Your parents love you and want to know when you're unhappy, and they'll probably have thoughts that will help. You could also talk to another adult you trust, such as a relative, a teacher, a school counselor, or a clergyperson if you attend religious services.

Dear Highlights,

the only Black kid in my class I am
and i fell left out and sometimes
i get bullied what Should i do.

—Jayden, 2019

Dear Jayden,

We strongly encourage you to talk to your parents about what's been going on and how you've been feeling. They care about you and want to know what's on your mind, and they may be able to offer you some helpful advice. You could also talk to your teacher privately about the bullying and how you've been feeling left out and uncomfortable. Remember your teacher is responsible for creating a classroom environment where everyone feels safe, comfortable, and ready to learn.

When people bully or exclude others, it reflects badly on them—not on the person they're bullying. Please try not to let your classmates' behavior affect the way you feel about yourself.

If there are a few classmates who seem friendly, you might try to talk with them so you can get to know them better. You might also look around for kids who might welcome a new friend.

If your classmates say unkind things, you could let them know how you feel. If you feel safe doing so, you could respond to a comment by saying, "Your comments are disrespectful, and I'd appreciate it if you didn't talk that way." While they might not change their behavior immediately, they'll probably think about what you said. You might also stay near a supervising adult. Kids are less likely to misbehave when an adult can see and hear what's going on.

In addition to talking to your parents and your teacher, you could talk to another adult you trust, such as a relative, a school counselor, or a clergyperson if you attend a place of worship. Remember, this isn't something you need to resolve on your own.

Dear Highlight's

I'm the only white person in my class. Everyone calls me a white cracker. I read your story about STAGE FRIGHT, It Kinda gave me some (2 or 3) ideas. What else can I do or say.

—Tina, age 11, 1999

Dear Tina,

Most people experience being in the minority (either for how they look or how they think or feel) at one time or another. Although we know you find it hard to be in this position, you may want to keep in mind that many of your classmates might feel this way whenever they go to a store or out of their neighborhood. Learning to see things from their point of view may help you make friends and learn to get along with others. Right now, you may find it hard to be the one who looks different on the outside, but you will probably realize that the truth is that everyone is the same on the inside.

The other kids in your class are teasing you by calling you a name you don't like. We get many letters from kids who are being teased. The first thing we suggest is that you talk to whoever is calling you names and let that person know that you don't wish to be called "white cracker." You would probably be surprised how many readers have written in to tell us they tried this, and it really helped.

If talking doesn't work, then we suggest that you try ignoring the teasers. People who tease others do so to get a response out of the person being teased. So, the hard fact is, the less you react to or even acknowledge the teasing, the less fun it will be to tease you and the less it will happen.

We know it is really hard to just ignore someone who is purposely being mean to you. Perhaps you can get a friend to help you. Whenever someone calls you that name, your friend can try to distract you from listening by telling you a funny story or by helping you get your mind on something else. This way, you'll be concentrating on what your friend is saying and won't even hear what is going on in the background. If you are alone when the teasing happens, you might want to try pulling out a book and reading it. Again, this may help by giving you something else to think about. These suggestions may be hard to do at first, but maybe you could give them a try or two and see if there is any change.

We also suggest that you talk to your parents or some other adult you trust about how you feel. They may have some suggestions or words of encouragement that may help you.

Dear Highlights,

I am an immigrant. I decided to do a report on immigrants in NC. I discovered an organization called ICE. I realized how badly immigrants were being treated in some places and wanted to know how I could help. Got any ideas?

—Anonymous, 2017

Dear Friend,

We're glad you wrote to us. We can tell you're a caring, compassionate person who wants to help others.

If you haven't already, we suggest that you talk this over with your parents. They will want to know how strongly you feel about this, and they may have some helpful thoughts to share with you. With your parents' guidance, you may want to contact some local organizations that assist immigrants in your area. Some community centers and places of worship may have soup kitchens, food pantries, homeless shelters, and clothing closets to help people in need.

If you want to write letters expressing your views about the laws concerning immigration, your parents can help you find the names and addresses of elected officials on the local, state, and national levels. You might also consider writing a letter to the editor of a local newspaper.

Letters About

COVID-19

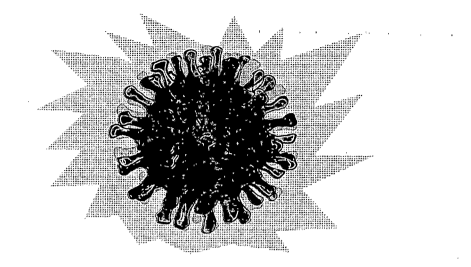

N OUR 75 YEARS OF CONVERSATIONS WITH *HIGHLIGHTS*
readers, many kids have shared their thoughts and feelings about
significant events that have shaped the U.S. and the world. These defining
moments leave an indelible impression on kids when they occur in their
formative years. They are the events kids remember all their lives—
the experiences that lead them as adults to ask one another the familiar
question, "Where were *you* when . . . ?"

Our archive holds letters from readers who have written about living in
the time of the Vietnam War, the assassination of President John F. Kennedy,
the civil rights movement, our early explorations into space, the horrific
events of 9/11 and war in the Middle East, the changing tide of LGBTQ+
rights, the Columbine shooting, the Boston Marathon bombing, and other
significant happenings. Although each of these events left its own distinctive
mark on the world, none was experienced at the same time, in largely the
same way, by people the world over. That's what occurred in 2020 with the
COVID-19 pandemic.

Reader mail about COVID-19 began trickling in almost as soon as directives to "stay safer at home" were issued. Interestingly, the first message we received was an email from YiYi, a reader in China. The reader wanted to visit a friend who would soon be moving, but wondered if it was safe.

Soon after, kids in the U.S. began writing to us as they grappled with the sudden, early closing of school and the beginning of distance learning. They wrote about the new practices of wearing masks and social distancing. Kids wrote to us asking for information. "What is COVID-19?" one child asked early in the pandemic via email. Other children wrote to express worry about friends and neighbors who didn't seem to be taking the precautions recommended by the Centers for Disease Control and Prevention (CDC). We received reader mail expressing concern for health-care professionals and other frontline workers. Minerva wrote, "My mom has a friend who is a nurse. A lot of men and women are risking their lives to save others. My mom is making reusable face masks."

Many children wrote looking for ideas of things to do. "It can get very boring around my house," one reader said. "I detest Quarantine! I have

These defining moments leave an indelible impression on kids when they occur in their formative years.

tried baking, ballet, games, swimming, bike riding, and playing outsides. What do I do?!?!" Giselle wrote a poem about quarantine, saying, "It feels like 100 years, and 100 years more. / When do I get to open my door?"

We listened, and we empathized in a way that we hadn't before. For the first time, we were confronting many of the same emotions as our readers, at the same place in time. Our adult circumstances—working from home, being unable to socialize with friends, missing milestone events, and feeling bored—were very similar to their experiences. "We're all in this together," was a popular slogan that we repeated to kids and kids repeated to us.

We listened, and we empathized in a way that we hadn't before. For the first time, we were confronting many of the same emotions as our readers, at the same place in time.

In almost every instance, we assumed that the letter writer had some degree of anxiety, even if it wasn't explicitly expressed. As always, the challenge was to address anxiety without heightening or adding to it. We reminded kids that many researchers were working around the clock to find treatments for the sick and that scientists were working to develop an effective vaccine. We advised them to follow the CDC guidelines to stay healthy—and we urged them to stay hopeful.

We were disappointed to be unable to offer definitive answers to some of the kids' questions, such as queries about the nature of the virus or the status of the new school year. At times, the information available to us seemed to change almost daily. But we could focus on presenting concrete ideas for staying engaged in productive activities, and we suggested ways kids could show sensitivity, compassion, and encouragement to others. Sometimes kids told us about their own ideas for helping. Violet, age 11, wrote to say that she was creating a website to support people suffering from COVID-related stress and asked for suggestions for ways to get the word out. Ten-year-old Ella wrote a poem urging kids to call someone on the phone and wear a smile.

Employing ideas of their own and making and taking suggestions from others, many kids were determined to help. Thanks to their efforts, those who were socially isolated in neighborhoods across the U.S. may have felt a little less lonely. The messages of kindness sent from kids were received in the mail, displayed on posters in front windows, delivered via video chat, and expressed in other creative ways.

It's too soon to know the long-term effect of the pandemic on kids. But when it all started and many months into it, kids led with empathy, showing what it means to be optimistic in the deepest sense of the word. With confidence, they leaned into their creativity and problem-solving skills to manage their confusion. Even the act of writing to *Highlights* for advice on alleviating boredom or adjusting to the many inconveniences of quarantine revealed a faith in themselves. It was evidence of their belief that feeling helpless in situations that may seem hopeless is counterproductive. Refusing to feel powerless, kids stepped up and showed their best selves.

THE LETTERS

Dear highlights, if the coronavirus is going around how do you make magazines???

—Khalil, age 9, 2020

Dear Khalil,

Like many other employees, the *Highlights* staff is working from home on computers. As you can imagine, it took us a little time to adjust to the change. But many people—including you, your family, and friends, we're sure—have had changes in their daily routine. This is a challenging time for all of us, but we'll get through it.

We are happy that the printers for our magazine are all working on schedule, too. So our readers will receive their issues on time.

We hope you are looking forward to receiving your next *Highlights* issue.

Dear Highlights,
During quarantine I am getting bored easily and I don't feel in the mood to do my schoolwork sometimes. A lot about this hard for me because I have a little sister.

Do you have any advice on how to be more positive about this?

—Vivian, 2020

Dear Highlights, .
I love your magazine so much! I look at them almost everyday. But I love reading the Dear Highlights. They give me idea of what to do if I have a similar problem. Now, here is my question.

Since I'm at home all the time now, how can I stay productive while doing my schoolwork?

Thank you!

—Mia, 2020

Stay Safe DURING COVID-19
We are in this together.

—Jacob, age 12, 2020

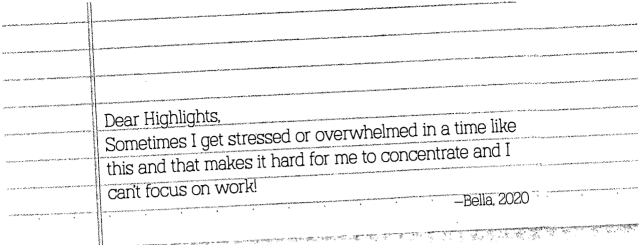

Dear Highlights,
Sometimes I get stressed or overwhelmed in a time like this and that makes it hard for me to concentrate and I can't focus on work!

—Bella, 2020

Dear Bella,

Many people find it helpful to work in "study blocks." If it's OK with your parents that you use this plan, set a timer for 20 minutes and use that time to focus on one class or assignment without distractions. Don't worry about rushing —just work until the timer goes off. Then, take a break for five to ten minutes. Walk around, stretch, get a glass of water or a snack, or chat with a family member. You might pop outside for a breath of fresh air. Then, when the break is over, study for another 20 minutes. Taking frequent breaks can help prevent you from getting overwhelmed or tired.

Also be sure to get plenty of healthy food, activity, and rest outside of your school hours. We suggest being firm with your schedule. If you go to bed and wake up at the same time each day, your mind and body will feel more prepared to take on the day. Take some time to move around daily—play games in the yard or do some yoga stretches. You might go on a walk with your parents if the weather is nice.

You can also ask your parents for more suggestions. They know just how busy you are, and we're sure they'll be happy to help you brainstorm some ways to keep organized. Perhaps you and your family can plan something fun to do together. You might have a family game night on Friday evenings, or you could set up a video chat with extended family. Having something to look forward to with your loved ones can also help keep you on track with your day-to-day responsibilities.

Be sure to talk to your parents, too, if you're feeling scared or worried. Sometimes just sharing your concerns with the people who love you can help ease your mind.

This is a challenging time for all of us, but we'll get through it.

Nothing Lasts Forever!

You might think School will never reopen

And you might just sit around mopeing

But I know better Nothing lasts forever!

—Eliza, age 11, 2020

Coronavirus

always something to do

Even know if the whole word is shut down
and being home is boring, there is always something
to do read a book, do the dishes, and if you Live on
a farm milk cows or feed calfs. (I do)

—Corbin, age 9, 2020

Dear Highlights,
I need an HONEST answer. Are we gonna go back to school before the end of the year? I am 11 and really wanna finish 5th grade. Can you give me an honest answer please?
—Anonymous, 2020

Dear Highlights,
All this talk about the corona virus is scaring me. I'm worried that I won't go to school next year. What is this stuff really about?
—Chloe, 2020

Dear Highlights,
So when the president said that we had to stay home I got to facetalk my friend Owen again and again does this mean we have to stay home forever?
—Andrew, 2020

Dear Andrew,

Thank you for your message. You aren't alone. Many kids wonder how long they will have to stay home because of the COVID-19 pandemic.

Although we have to stay home for now, it won't be forever. But we don't know how long it will be. No one has all the answers right now. Government officials, schoolteachers and principals, business owners, employees, parents, and kids like you are all trying to do the best they can with the information they have. Because COVID-19 is new and we've never had to deal with it before, we're all learning as we go along. It can be frustrating, we know, but all we can do is follow the guidelines and be patient.

We encourage you to talk to your parents about how you're feeling. Your parents can help ease your mind. With their permission, you could continue to stay in contact with Owen and your other friends by talking on the phone, emailing, and video chatting.

If you are doing classes at home, focus on your work and continue to be the best student you can be. Set up a routine so that you stay on track. If you are not doing classes at home, assign yourself some work! Reading, practicing math, and working on projects can help keep your mind sharp. In your free time, you could make crafts, bake, do puzzles, organize your room, or work on a new hobby you've always wanted to try.

This is a challenging time for all of us, but we'll get through it.

Dear Highlights, there are some cases of coronavirus in Fairbanks and my cousin came back from out of state how can I not worry about it.

—Avery, age 8, 2020

Dear Highlights,
We are very stressed about all of the news on coronavirus. Help!

—Grace, age 10, 2020
—Aubrey, age 13, 2020

Dear Highlights,
When I first heard about the pandemic that is stealing many lives of people, I was mad. Though recently I was scared about this whole pandemic thing and it is very scary. How should I feel about this?

Please help me understand this pandemic.

–Gwen, 2020

Dear Gwen,

Keeping your feelings bottled up inside can be stressful. We encourage you to talk to your parents about your fears. They are the best ones to guide you whenever you have questions or just need someone to talk to. Your parents especially want to know if you're feeling scared, angry, or unsure. They can help ease your mind. It might also help to think about all the people—doctors, nurses, and other health-care workers—who are doing their very best to treat those who have the virus. And there are many scientists working to create a vaccine. Thinking about the helpers in times of trouble often makes us feel less worried, and it might help you feel better, too.

Although it's good to be aware of what is going on in the world, sometimes watching the news too often can be overwhelming. Even if there's new information, the reports often repeat many things that have been said before. Hearing the same alerts over and over again can be alarming and cause us to feel more stressed every time we hear them. So, it can be good to limit the time you spend watching and listening to the news.

We encourage you to focus on the things you enjoy. Reading books, making crafts, baking, doing puzzles, organizing your room, and doing your schoolwork if you have assignments now are all positive, productive things to do. With your parents' permission, you could also stay in contact with your friends and relatives by talking on the phone, emailing, and video chatting.

Finally, remember to take good care of yourself by getting enough sleep, exercising, and eating healthy meals and snacks. You can encourage your friends and family to do the same.

Dear Highlights,
My dad's a Dr. He tells me to stay HOME!! But, sometimes, we ride bikes with masks, and are neighbor, Gemma. We keep a distance of 10 feet. It's hard sometimes, but at least we can play. Some kids in are neighborhood still play, go inside others home, and play with the same ball. It's not fair, but we are staying safe. So it's fine. We are making signs with water for Dr. 'Cause sometimes it's warm, sometimes it's cold, in PA. Weave 'bin doing drive by's.

—Paige, 2020

Dear Paige,
I'm glad that you are following your dad's instructions. After all, he's a doctor, and he knows a lot about staying healthy!

All of us at *Highlights* are social distancing right now, too, by working from home. Like you, many of us live in Pennsylvania, where the weather is sometimes warm and sometimes cold. Today happens to be a warm day with plenty of sunshine.

It's nice that you are able to go for bike rides with your neighbor Gemma while still keeping some distance between you. It's not an ideal situation, I know, but it's great that you can spend some time together.

Take care, Paige. We'll get through this! All of us at *Highlights* wish you, your family, and Gemma the best.

Dear Highlights,
My name is Troy. I am 8 years old. Because we are stuck inside during this scary time, I decided to help kids have a little fun. I created a YouTube channel with daily challenges, tricks and comedy. I hope you like it and share it with others.

—Troy, age 8, 2020

Dear Troy,
Thank you for sending us the link to your YouTube channel. We enjoyed seeing your daily challenges and tricks. You have a great imagination and sense of humor!

You sound like a caring person, Troy, and we're glad to have you as a reader and a friend.

Crazy People

The coronavirus
has made everyone crazy.
Pantries are filed with toilet paper,
rice, and beans
that no one knows how to cook.
And people barricaded indoors
not able to see friends.
Scared for their lives.
Learning to have faith.

—Dorian, 2020

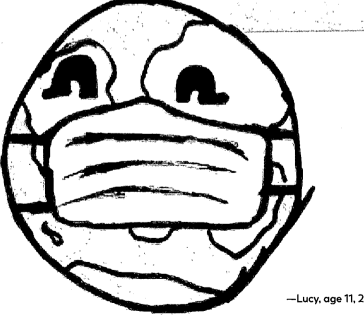

—Lucy, age 11, 2020

Dear highlights,
I am 9 and I live in Chattanooga TN.
I need your advice. Covid-19 virus
is hard because nobody in My neighbo-
-rhood seems to care. Nobody understand.
social-distency. My best freinds don't even
care. I need help. What do I do?

—Brooklyn, age 9, 2020

Dear Brooklyn,

We're sorry that your best friends and neighbors don't seem to understand the need for social distancing right now. It's important that everyone follow the safety guidelines so that we lessen the spread of the coronavirus.

We encourage you to talk this over with your parents. Explain that you are concerned about your best friends' and neighbors' actions during this time. Your parents can help ease your mind.

It's important to realize that you can't control what other people do, but you can control what you do. If your neighbors and best friends want to play, explain that you can't do that right now, but you'll be happy to play with them again once the restrictions have been lifted. You can say that you will talk on the phone, email, or video chat with them, if your parents say it's OK. If your best friends and neighbors argue with you, you can simply say, "I just want all of us to stay healthy," and then go inside.

We encourage you to focus on the things you enjoy. Reading books, making crafts, baking, doing puzzles, organizing your room, and doing your schoolwork if you have assignments now are all positive, productive things to do.

Finally, remember to take good care of yourself by getting enough sleep and eating healthy meals and snacks. You can encourage your friends and family to do the same.

COVID 19

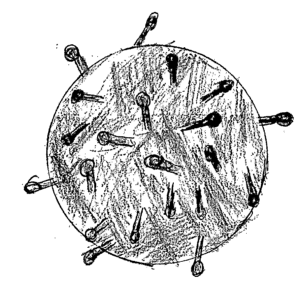

It doesn't bother me

Not my friends or family either
But the city is big & dirty
So there's lots of disease there

—Abigail, age 10, 2020

Quarentine

Quarentine! Oh, quarentine!

Oh, how so awfully bad!

I don't want to stay at home!

It makes me very sad!

Quarentine! Oh, quarentine!

I wish you would go away!

Go away so everyone,

Can hang with friends and play

—Sofia, age 11, 2020

Coronavirus Concerns

kids, Corona virus, and Concerns are changing the way we learn. I still love to read, write, and learn but at this moment it is a real concern. Math is not my favorite lesson it's no confession my mom's the teacher and this is a feature she's' a permanet guest reader. Work and play all day but I still love shool anyway.

—Ashlynn, age 9, 2020

Dear Highlights,

Hi, You may already know me because I sent a ton of letters to you when I was younger. I'm 12 years old know but I'm turning 13 on May 4th. I know it's great an all—I'm becoming a 'teenager and there will be new opportunities—but it's not going to be very exciting. Thanks to the coronavirus, I'm not allowed to have anyone over. It's just going to be... lonely. I know there are people out there who have it much worse than me, but I've been so excited to turn 13 and now I can't even be around those I love. Of course, my immediate family will be here, but they're always very busy and I don't want to bother them. The only one that isn't busy is my sister _____. But she couldn't care less about me (she likes me but she's 14 months old sooo...).

I know you probably have better things to do but I wasn't sure who to talk to. I don't want my parents to have to stress over me with all the other things on their minds. Same goes for my friends. So I decided to ask you since you always give great advice. How can I cheer myself up?

Thank you for your time.

—Lyla, age 12, 2020

Dear Lyla,

We're glad you decided to write to us about this. It's OK to feel disappointed that your birthday celebration won't be the way you had hoped it would be. It's important to acknowledge feelings, even feelings of disappointment. You seem to be a good writer, one who can express herself well. You might want to write down your feelings to get them off your chest. Sometimes just putting your sad feelings down on paper is a good way to think them through and let them go.

You might talk to your parents about the possibility of having a birthday party with your relatives and friends once the COVID-19 safe-distancing restrictions have been lifted. Many people are having to reschedule special events—even weddings. So, rescheduling your birthday party may be an option. And for now, you could ask your parents if your family could have a special meal and a cake on your birthday or the following weekend. Even though your sister is only 19 months old, we're sure she would be thrilled to help you blow out the candles on your cake—and, of course, help you eat it!

Although you won't be able to see your friends and relatives face-to-face on your birthday, you could phone them, email them, or video chat, if your parents say it's OK. Give people the chance to share your special day and all the excitement that goes along with turning 13.

We all wish you a very happy birthday and a year filled with joy!

Dear A,
I always miss my friends on the weekends and the coronavirus is like an extra-long weekend and I don't know what to do. Any suggestion.

Love,
—Macy, 2020

Dear Highlights,
During this time, I'm around my family a lot. What are some fun things we can do together without leaving the house or yard?
                —Carly, age 12, 2020

Dear Highlights,
I'm stuck at home with nothing to do but nothing. Do you have any suggestions?

—Zach, 2020

Dear Zach,

Thank you for your message. As we're sure you know, you're not alone in this situation. Many other kids are also at home during this time. We're glad to see that you want to find some fun things to keep yourself busy. Having a positive and productive attitude is an excellent approach to your unexpected time at home!

Having goals can keep you on track. For instance, you could challenge yourself to write one poem every day for two weeks straight. Or you might practice drawing objects around the house—try to draw everything on your desk or bedroom dresser, for example. If you get bored, take a break and work on a different project. Then, later on, come back to the first one. If you keep your goals in mind while working on these projects, you may find it easier to focus on them and have fun.

You could also try learning something new. Is there a recipe you've always wanted to make? Have you tried making crafts with recycled objects? Or have

you tried a new exercise, such as yoga? You could even design your own robot or learn how to plant a seed garden. With a parent's permission, you could do some research online or look for fun activities.

Another idea is to help out around the house. You could offer to do the dishes, take out the trash, or clean out the fridge or a closet. Put on your favorite music or audiobook and tackle each task. We're sure your parents will be very grateful for the help—and it can also help your home feel fresh and new!

We encourage you to ask your parents for suggestions, too. We're sure they'll be happy to help you brainstorm some good ideas. They can also help you find the best way to balance your daily schedule, including your schoolwork, if you have any. It's important to support your family during this time—and just as important to rely on them when you need to. Be sure to talk to them often and let them know how you're feeling. You might even involve them in your projects and activities.

christine, I have
a ~~Ask~~ Arizona ~~Problem~~ problem that
I need help fixing!
I am felling Down lately
and I miss my friends.
Got andy tips?

— Down in Denver

I hope you/Arizona can
Help me. Thanks!

—Ella, 2020

Dear Highlights,
I just turned 6. I was going to have an America's Got talent
Party. But my party was cancelled cause of the Carona shut
down. I miss everyone.

—Sylvie, 2020

Dear Highlights,
I'm having a really hard time adjusting to social distancing and I miss my friends. Have any tips?
—Makayla, age 11, 2020

Dear Highlights,
i miss my friends and i can't see them any more. i'm sad
—Willow, 2020

Dear Makayla,

We understand how much you must miss your friends right now. We're sure they miss you, too! But for now, we all must follow the social distancing guidelines so we can help limit the spread of COVID-19.

Even though you can't see your friends face-to-face right now, there are probably other ways you can keep in touch. With your parents' permission, you could video chat with your friends, talk on the phone, or exchange emails or text messages. You could write a story together by email: one of you writes the first paragraph, the next person writes the second paragraph, and so on until the story is finished.

Then you could each illustrate the story separately. Perhaps your parents can help you share the illustrations with your friends electronically. It will be fun to see how each of you interprets the story through your artwork.

Ask your parents for more ideas on activities you and your friends can do without playing together in person. You and your family might plan some fun things you can do together while social distancing, such as having a family game night, trying new recipes, or having a silly dance contest.

We hope this helps, Makayla. This is a challenging time for all of us, but we'll get through it.

Hope

Even though the world is shut down,
in every city, and every town,
We will hold onto hope,
There is no time to mope,
we must be as strong as we can,
just like every other child, woman, and man
and hopefully soon, things will get better,
and we might even find some toilet paper.

—Ava, age 13, 2020

we're in this together

We're in this together,
I'm here for you.
There may have
been a pamdimic
or two, there may
have been three
~~tropical storms or~~
Even Riots becoming
large. but we're in
this together, I'm
here for you. so
can we take a
second or two
to realize,
I'm here
for you.

—Abigail, age 11, 2020

—Joelin, age 9, 2020

Really
Hard
Things

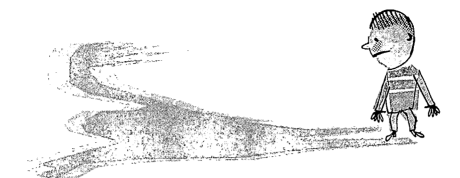

ADULTS SOMETIMES CLING TO THE NOTION OF AN idyllic, carefree childhood. We want to pretend that misfortune or unpleasant events don't or won't happen to children. The reality is, of course, that childhood is often fraught with hard things. When a hard thing crops up in our kids' lives, it triggers in us an instinct to protect them or fix the problem. In most cases, this urge doesn't add to our efforts to raise kids who are resilient. As difficult as it is for parents not to rush in to rescue, kids need to experience some hard things to understand they can get through them. Or, as Franklin D. Roosevelt said, "A smooth sea never made a skilled sailor."

The vast majority of letters and emails that we receive from children asking for advice describe circumstances they are likely to weather without serious consequences. For example, they write to us about the death of a beloved pet, the very real challenges of moving or changing schools, and about friends treating them cruelly. Events like these are certainly unpleasant and often very difficult. But kids, with the help of supportive adults, can eventually absorb the learnings embedded in each experience and move on, while becoming more resilient and more capable.

Even the more difficult trials kids write to us about, one generation after another, often concern the losses and disappointments most of us face at one time or another: a grandparent's death, a serious illness in the family, a loss of household income, and even the separation, divorce, and remarriage of a parent. These events (addressed in other chapters) are significant and distressing when they happen, and they may be forever remembered. In most cases, however, they are not likely to prevent kids from leading happy, successful lives.

But some kids are faced with *really* hard things—challenges they can manage only with extensive adult intervention. Even then, the pain can be crippling. And the experiences can leave permanent scars.

But some kids are faced with *really* hard things—challenges they can manage only with extensive adult intervention.

These are the children who linger longer in our minds and hearts—the kids who write to us about problems with both short- and long-term consequences—about trauma that can have a lifelong effect. These are the children who write to confide that their parents or older siblings are physically harming them or have substance abuse problems that affect them. They write to us about mental illness in the family—or share their own depression or suicidal thoughts. They tell us about their struggles with eating disorders and their self-harming behaviors, such as cutting. In the last decade or so, some kids have told us how they are rethinking their gender identity or sexual orientation and about their fear of being ostracized or ridiculed if they are open about it.

The fear of being ridiculed is powerful, and we often lament the sad fact that kids (and adults) can sometimes be cruel. As our mail has reminded us for decades, few children pass through childhood without being teased. Maybe they are needled about their appearance, their name, their disabilities or abilities, or their quirky or "clueless" fashion sense. Sometimes they never know why they are picked on. Teasing, however, usually has a temporary quality to it, and we can urge kids to ignore it and even suggest tactics that can help stop it. But when teasing persists or when it escalates to bullying—physically harming or threatening someone—an adult must step in. Despite anti-bullying campaigns that gained popularity in schools after the Columbine shooting in 1999, bullying persists.

The kids who are targets of bullies today are no different from the kids who were targets of bullies years ago. The letter we received 40 years ago from seven-year-old Jeremy, who reported that he was bullied because he was "fat and wears glasses," could have easily been written by a different child in every decade since. Kids often tell us that they've talked to adults, but they don't feel safer. They ask, "What should I do?" "Why is this happening?" "Can you help?" Keith, the target of a class bully in 2006, wrote, "I try to ignore him, but he doesn't stop. I want to make a wish that he will stop, but my birthday isn't soon. What should I do?"

We also hear about bullying based on race, religion, or sexual orientation. These topics are probably more prevalent among teens, but *Highlights* readers also experience them, as seen in our mail over the years. In 1995, Sadie wrote, "Kids make fun of me because I'm Korean. They give me threats and call me names. The neighbors' kids make prank phone calls and make fun of my family." In 2020, Nora wrote, "The kids in my class bully me sometimes because of the color of my skin. I'm also really stressed out because I'm going into 6th grade and they make it even harder for me. Please help me." While this kind of taunting used to happen primarily in school, on the playground, or in backyards, in the 2000s, taunting found another home—on the internet. Extreme insensitivity or outright cruelty from others is one of the *really* hard things likely to leave a lasting impression on kids, influencing the way they see themselves and sometimes altering their course in life. Indeed, sometimes it leads to severe anxiety, self-harming behaviors, or even suicide.

> Extreme insensitivity or outright cruelty from others is one of the *really* hard things likely to leave a lasting impression on kids, influencing the way they see themselves and sometimes altering their course in life.

We never have enough information in a letter or email to fully understand the depth of a child's despair—we can only respond to what they tell us. But we take every request for help or advice seriously, seeking the counsel of credentialed professionals to ensure that we are answering these serious letters in the best possible way. It happens rarely, but when necessary, we report likely abuse or neglect to authorities, as required by law. More often, to err on the side of caution, we find ourselves offering kids hotline numbers for suicide prevention and child abuse and neglect. With fervent hope that they'll follow through, we always urge these kids to find and talk to a trusted adult right away.

For many kids, childhood isn't the short, sweet season it's meant to be. Events, seldom of their own making, lead kids to feeling as one reader in 2014 did. A child being raised by her father and sisters with no mother in her life, she described herself as "depressed . . . worthless and like I should die . . . nasty . . ." She went on, "But that's not me. I'm really quiet, joyful, and kind. But I think that me is almost gone like I'm trapped in a dark cave and my torch is burning out."

Let's work to keep the torches of kids in darkness brightly lit.

Dear Highlights,
My dad drinks too much. I have talked to the school counselor. She said I should try to get him into a clinic that helps people who have a drinking problem. But I couldn't get him in there if I had to. What do I do?

—M. S., 1992

Dear M. S.,

Speaking with a counselor is a good idea. If your dad isn't willing to get help, ask the counselor about help for yourself, such as the program Alateen, where you could talk with others your age who face a similar problem. Can you talk with your mom? She may be able to help also. We know that you want very much to help your father and to make him stop. Perhaps you can tell him how his drinking makes you feel. He may not realize how much it is hurting you. Hiding how you feel and pretending things are fine will not help him or you. It's also important for you to realize that his drinking is not something you can control. He has to decide to stop for himself. Some people behave very differently when they drink. If your father does, you should know that it has nothing to do with you and that you are not responsible for it. It is due to his drinking. You may feel better if you can talk this over with someone you trust—perhaps a teacher, an adult whom you know in a church or synagogue, or a relative.

Dear Highlights,
I have a problem unlike ones in your magazine. My parents don't know I'm contacting you for help but I hate myself. I harm myself and feel fat. I think I might have anorexia. My parents don't know and I need help but don't want to go to a mental hospital... Help me please. Thanks.

–Anonymous, 2013

Dear Friend,

We urge you to talk with your parents or another adult you trust right away so you can get the help you need. A trusted adult could be a relative, the mother of a friend, a school counselor, or a clergyperson if you attend religious services. Talking with a caring adult can help you to think about things in new ways and come up with solutions to things that are bothering you. If you'd like to talk to someone anonymously, you can call 1-800-442-4673. You will talk with a counselor who can help you work through how you're feeling. You can call this number day or night. If you call from a landline (not a cell phone), the call is toll-free and will not appear on your phone bill.

It might help you to know that you're not alone in feeling insecure about your body. We hear from so many readers who worry about the way they look—about being too short, too tall, too fat, too skinny, even too "average." But the truth is that diversity is a big part of what makes the world beautiful. We hope you will learn to accept the person you are and come to appreciate your body for the wonderful thing that it is!

We hope you'll also try to make healthy choices in general when it comes to your body. If you treat your body with respect and love—by eating well-balanced meals (not skipping any!), exercising regularly, getting enough rest, and refraining from dangerous behaviors that might harm your body, we believe your mind will begin to feel better, too. A doctor could offer you some helpful advice on good ways to take care of your body.

You might find that writing in a journal can be a good way to get some worries off your chest. Try making a list of things you like about yourself, as well as nice events happening in your life. Keep this list in a handy place so that you can read it often and add a new item to the list every day. It would also be a good idea to do the things you enjoy more often. Focusing on positive things will help you to enjoy life more.

Over the years, we've found that true beauty is always worn "inside-out." That is, it shines through a person's kind words and thoughtful actions. We are lucky to have many readers who possess this type of beauty. We're confident that you're one of them!

Do Editor

I have a family problem, I am 11
and my sisters 7. My parents argue all
the time and one of them might leave.
Even one time my Mom threw a plate at
my Dad, I got really scared. And sometimes
my Dad gets drunk and hit me. What should
I do?   GOD help me please
                         please
                         please

Very
    sincerly

        (☺)

        Social Studies   teacher
            ↓   ↓   ↓

Dear Mr. Editor, ____ does have
family problems. Try to help him.
                        Thank you.

—Rick, age 11, 1976

Dear Rick,

Your letter distresses
us very much and
we wish there was
something we could
do to help other than
just give advice.
You must try very
hard to understand
that others have
problems also. Your
sister needs your
help; being younger
means she is less
able to understand
than you are. Work
hard in school
and try to keep
busy in school
activities. Then some of the problems you have may
not seem as important.

Since you are obviously a religious young man,
keep your faith and we are sure you will get comfort
from it. It may not seem so right now, but these
problems will pass. If you want to write to us at any
time, we will always be glad to hear from you.

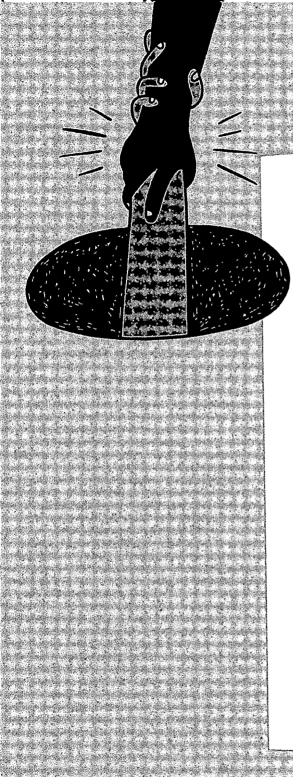

I keep falling.
It's not getting better.
No matter what I do,
I can't fix it.
My depression is bad.
It takes over me.
No matter what I do,
I keep falling.
My hole is more than 6 ft deep.
I hate it,
It is not so sleek.
This hole of mine.
Pulling me out will take some time.
Until I met you.
You pulled me out.
I am doing fine now.
I am not falling.

—Thomas, age 12, 2018

Bullys

There is a group of 5th graders who are always
picking on someone or beating them up. I want to stand
up for them but the are a lot of them and there stronger
then me. If I tell on them they will beat me up.
I ask my parents if I could take kerate but they
don't have veary much money. Please help!

—Jackson, 2003

Dear Jackson,

We hope you will talk to your parents about what is happening at school. Your parents love you very much, and they want what's best for you. We're sure they will want to know about anything that's bothering you. They may have some useful ideas for you. We also hope you will tell your parents that you are concerned that the bullies may beat you up if you tell. That may help your parents decide how to handle the situation in a way that keeps you safe.

We think you are right that there are too many bullies for you to fight with them. If there is a martial artist who can fight off three or more people at once, then that person has been training hard for many years, not the few months that you have left in the school year.

Here are some tips that we have adapted from the advice of medical experts:

Put safety first. If you think you are in physical danger or if a bully has already pushed, hit, or kicked you, don't be afraid to ask an adult for help.

Talk about your feelings. Sometimes just talking about what you're going through can make you feel better. Talk to your parent, teacher, guidance counselor, coach, or another trusted adult. A caring adult can give you some good advice and may be able to protect you if you are in danger.

Walk tall with your head held high. This sends a message to bullies that you feel good about yourself and that you're not afraid. If you do not look like an "easy mark," they are more likely to leave you alone.

Ignore the bullies or pretend they don't exist. Bullies are usually trying to get attention. They want certain reactions from you. If you don't react at all, it may not be fun for the bullies, and they may just give up.

Take a stand by speaking up. Sometimes just saying things like, "Leave me alone" or "Stop calling me that name" can help.

If possible, stay in a group. Bullies are usually much less brave if you are with a friend or two.

Don't use physical force to deal with a bully. There's no way to tell ahead how a bully may react if he or she feels threatened.

You can be brave without getting into a fight. Bullying is a tough problem, and there is probably not one single solution that will end each case of bullying. We hope you will keep talking to the adults you trust about how you feel and how you can keep yourself and others safe. Remember that talking to an adult is not "tattling" when someone has been hurt or could be hurt.

Dear Highlights,

I am 11, a girl, and I have two loving parents. The only problem is, I think I like girls and boys. I've been thinking this for a while now, since about 3rd grade, but I'd just brush it off. I don't know what to do, and how to tell my parents. Can you help me?

—Anonymous, age 11, 2016

Dear Friend,

We can see that you're concerned about the feelings you have, but you might try not to worry about it for now. Try to remember that you'll have plenty of time later in life to have romantic relationships. Now is a good time to form meaningful friendships and participate in activities you enjoy.

We noticed you described your parents as loving. That leads us to believe that you have a great relationship with them. We encourage you to talk to them about the things that are on your mind. Your parents love you and want to know what you're going through, and they might have some good thoughts. We understand it can be awkward, though, to talk about personal things like this. You might choose a time when your parents aren't busy and say something such as, "I have something I'd like to talk to you about. Is now a good time?" If it is, you can tell them what you told us.

My aunt died recently in a car accident. I haven't seen my uncle since the accident. He is coming over soon. I'm not sure how I should act towards him. What should I do?

—Jessica, age 12, 1991

Dear Jessica,

There are no words to say to someone in your uncle's situation that will comfort him. When someone very close to you dies suddenly, it often takes a while for the shock to wear off and the reality to set in—you're not going to be talking and laughing and having fun with that person anymore. That's a lot to accept, and, depending on your uncle's nature, it may take a very long time for him to work through the anger, guilt, sadness, and loneliness that are a part of the grieving process.

It's difficult to say how you should act toward your uncle when we're not sure what your relationship was like before the accident. However, in general, your behavior should be supportive of him and of his feelings. He may need extra hugs, he may need to cry in front of the family, he might need to be very quiet, or he might need to talk. It's not necessary to say the perfect words that will make him feel better. Nothing but time and the love of those around him will ease the pain of losing his wife.

It might be difficult for you to see your uncle feeling bad. Grief is hard to watch, especially when you can't make it better. Try not to be afraid of it. If you can be a friend to your uncle, if you can look him in the eyes and let him see that you are sorry and that you'll miss your aunt, too, it will mean a lot to him.

Sometime, Jessica, if you want to, you can write down some of your memories of your aunt—good, bad, happy, sad, funny—and give them to your uncle. It's always nice to remember a person who has been a part of your life, so that a little part of them lives on with you.

Dear Highlights,

There's a girl at my school who's very strange. Everybody picks on her, and I learned that her parents died. She cuts herself and talks about how she doesn't belong on earth. I think she's going to commit suicide, and I'm scared to talk to her. I already talked to adults and my friends-it didn't help. I'm embarrassed to admit that I don't want to be her friend - just a guide through her tough times. And I'm scared for her. I witness some of her bullying, and she knows I'm there. She hates me already and she doesn't even know my name. I'm petrified and don't know what to do. How can I help her? *write back so fast ur thumbs bleed plz!

—Kate, 2013

Dear Kate,

You mentioned that you've already talked to adults and friends but it didn't help. If you haven't already talked to your parents, we urge you to do so right away. We also encourage you to talk with a school counselor, principal, teacher, and school nurse. These people can get this girl the help she needs.

You mentioned that this girl hates you and you're afraid to talk to her. We understand your hesitation to talk to her one-on-one. But please keep confiding in adults who can help this girl stay safe. Although you might not be able to help her directly, alerting people to the seriousness of this girl's condition is the right thing to do.

If you decide you do want to talk to her, you can encourage her to call 1-800-442-4673. She will talk with a counselor who is trained to advise children who are going through a tough time. She can call this number day or night. If she calls from a landline (not a cell phone), the call is toll-free and will not appear on her phone bill.

Divorce

You pray they come back.
But, they never come back.
You cry and cry because of fighting.
You're scared.
You cry and cry for the person you love to come back.
And now your family is split up and can never be a
family again.
Soon you have a step dad or a step mom.
Your family is split up.
What can you do?
Nothing to do.
Sadness is near you. Dad visits once a year or once a
month and
when he visits you hear screaming. This will scare you
for life.
Divorce hurts.

—Sophia, 2008

—Ellora, age 12, 2020

Smoking

My sister and I
hate when our
parents smoke.
We keep asking
them to STOP and
They say yes. But
They start to smoke
again. Whenever
They Take their lighter
we know they are going
To smoke. We always
try to blow it out.
Can you tell us
how they can stop
smoking?

—Claire, 1983

Dear Claire,

We understand that you and your sister are concerned about your parents smoking. However, this is not a decision that you can make for your parents. We realize that you are concerned for their health, but it is up to them to decide whether they want to smoke or not. You have been honest with them about your feelings. We think that is the most you can do.

We know that it is sometimes tempting to try to make people do what we want them to, especially when we feel that it is for their own good, but this is not a workable possibility. Everyone has to decide what is best for themselves. Everyone is responsible for him or herself. You can make the decision not to smoke, but you cannot make a decision for someone else. We know this is hard to accept, but you must. If your parents do quit smoking, you can be very supportive and helpful to them. Until then, however, try not to bug them too much even though it is tempting.

Dear Highlights,
I'm trans, but my family doesn't believe me. How do I make them understand that this is real?
—Roberto, 2016

Dear Roberto,

It's good that you want to be open with your family. They love you and want to know what's on your mind. You didn't mention which family members don't believe you, but sometime when things are quiet around the house, you might say something like, "I'd like to talk to you about something. Is now a good time?" Beginning a conversation like this is a good way to let the person know that what you're about to say is important to you.

It's good to realize, though, that conversations like this usually aren't just "one and done." Because you want your family members to understand you and you want to understand them, it will be helpful to keep the lines of communication open. When you talk together, make eye contact, speak calmly, and be willing to listen patiently without interrupting. The more often you can have openhearted talks together, the better your relationship may be.

You could also speak to a school guidance counselor. He or she might be able to offer some good feedback, and sometimes it helps just to talk things through. Writing in a journal is also a good way to figure out how to express what's on your mind.

Dear Highlights,

I want to help a girl whose name is Elizabeth. She doesn't have any friends, and I've heard that she wants to go to Chile to live with her grandparents because she feels lonely and left out here in Panama, where I live. To be totally honest, not really any of the girls have tried to be friendly to her, and she is kind of babyish. All the boys think she's disgusting, and that's sort of true, too.

Well, I've also heard something that has really scared me. Me and my friends have noticed that she wears make-up while none of the girls at school do; it's not allowed. We've found out that the reason for that is because her big brother, whose name is Ricardo, beats her up a lot, and she gets lots of bruises on her face, so she covers them up with make-up.

I don't like Elizabeth, but I really feel sorry for her. If I try to be friendly to her, I will also become like Gregorio; I won't have any friends left (except my best friend, whose name is Kendra). What should I do?

—Lily, 1999

Dear Lily,

This kind of decision is the hardest to make. On the one hand, you want to do the right thing, but on the other hand, you're afraid of what will happen. Unfortunately, the right choice isn't always the easy choice. However, you'll often find that once you make the right choice, the bad things that you worried about never happen. The fact is that you don't know how other people will react if you are friendly with Elizabeth. There are many things you can't control about the future. But you can be sure that if you behave in a way that you are proud of, you will feel better about yourself. Here's another way to look at it: Are friends who stop talking to you because you are kind to someone who needs help really friends? Making the right choice takes courage, but the reward of knowing you did the right thing is worth it.

If Elizabeth is getting beaten up, she needs adult help. If you talk to her, I urge you to encourage her to go to an adult she trusts, such as a relative, a teacher, a school counselor, a school nurse, or a clergyperson to ask for help. If she doesn't get help from the first person she asks, she should keep trying until someone helps her.

Cancer is bad.

Cancer is bad. It makes me mad! I am her nurse, I do my chores and help her more! I Love her so much, but she is so tough that's my mom!

—Carmen, age 8, 2008

Dear Highlights,

Please I beg you, give me a solution! My grandma and ma are mad at each other! They are fighting over who will leave! Grandma keeps hitting me because I don't listen to her (a good reason)! My mom says that it's wrong hitting people (like me)! I'm the one who them in this mess, Please help me!

—Kevin, age 8, 2007

Dear Kevin,

We're sorry to hear that this is happening. We don't agree that you got your mother and grandmother into this mess. They are adults and are responsible for what they do.

However, we're sorry to hear that you don't listen to your grandmother. We think we need to respect people. If you treat your grandmother as you would like to be treated and speak to her politely and considerately, then you may find that you can get along better with her. Your grandmother may feel that because she is the eldest, she has the authority to tell you what to do. If this makes a conflict for you, then we think it would be a good idea to talk it over with your mother and ask her advice.

If your grandmother hits you on your head and shoulders or hits you hard enough to leave bruises, then it's important to let your mother or another adult you trust, such as a teacher or school counselor, know right away. If you don't have anyone else to talk to, you can call the National Youth Crisis hotline at 1-800-442-4673. You will talk with a counselor who is trained to advise children with family problems. You can call this number day or night. The call is confidential and will not appear on your phone bill.

Dear Highlights,

I think I have depression. I have all the symptoms. I don't want to tell anyone because my mom will take me to many different doctors, but I know my mom causes it. She makes me sad every day. Sometimes she is so nice, but more often than not she's angry. She has slapped me in the face before because she said I deserved it, and dragged me by my hair. I am still angry and sad about that even though she has apologized. I am 12. I know I'm a bit old for highlights, but I would read it a lot when I was younger, and have always loved it. I thought of you when I need someone to talk to after I saw the symptoms of depression and realized the were so familiar. I don't know what to do.

–Anonymous, age 12, 2013

My Dad

Feb. 6 My dad died. The hour ... him. Nothing feels right around our house. Nothing feels the same. Every time I do some thing, I relized that I did it with my dad. These pains are coming on me harder than I thought.

—Rachel, age 9, 1990

Dear Rachel,

We are very sorry that your dad died. It takes a long time for family members to get over the loss of a loved one. Things will never go back to being the way they were—that would be impossible. But in time the pain that you are feeling now and the constant thoughts of your father will lessen, and you will once again be able to enjoy yourself and your home.

We think you are taking a step in the right direction when you write down your feelings, as you did in your letter to us. Writing our thoughts, especially when we are sad or upset, seems to have a healing effect. You might consider writing about the good memories you have of your father and the things you did together. Or you could just keep a journal of your thoughts and feelings as you go through the grieving process. If you keep writing in a notebook, you could write a dedication to your father on the inside cover, just as authors dedicate their books.

One other thing that might help is to think of how your father would want you and your family to be right now. He would probably want you to miss him, but would he really want you to all be miserable or to go ahead with your lives and be the best people you can be? Think of what an honor that would be to him.

Dear Highlights,

My brother keeps touching my privates. Every one in my individual family is repeatedly asking him to stop and he won't stop. But the thing is he's old enough to know better! Help!

—Allie, 2019

Dear Allie,

We're sorry this is happening. We're proud of you for reaching out and asking for help.

No one should touch you in a way that makes you feel uncomfortable. We encourage you to sit down with your parents and have a heart-to-heart talk with them. Explain you're very upset because your brother continues to touch you inappropriately. Tell them you want it to stop. Ask them for their help.

You didn't mention how old your brother is. If he is very young, he may enjoy the attention he gets from you and other family members when he touches you. We encourage you to firmly say, "Stop. This is my body, and you may not touch it that way," and move away

from him. Tell your parents or another supervising adult right away about what happened if they didn't see it.

If your brother isn't very young or if he's older than you, stay away from him and do not be alone with him. Be sure to tell your parents whenever he tries to touch you. If he continues to act this way, tell another trusted adult, such as a coach, Scout leader, or parent of a close friend. It's not tattling to protect yourself from being hurt and being touched inappropriately. Also, you can call 1-800-442-4673 to talk with a counselor who is trained to advise children who are in situations like the one you described. You can call this number day or night.

Dear Highlights,

Hi! I am 10 years old. I read a lot of your books and I have a promblem. My brother Phein keeps on hitting me and it harts. I tell him to stop. But he posent care. I tell my mom and Dad but they don't care either. Plese help me

—Nina, age 10, 1999

Dear Highlights,

I am 10½ years old and I hate myself and feel like commiting suicide.

—Brandy, age 10, 2000

Dear Brandy,

We hope you know that killing yourself is never an answer to any kind of problem or sadness. There is no situation in the world so bad that it can't be improved if you make an effort to work it out and ask for help in doing that.

We strongly urge you to talk with your parents about how you feel. They need to know when you're having trouble dealing with your feelings so they can help you work through them. You might start your conversation by saying something like, "This is hard for me to talk about, but I've been feeling very sad lately. I have even thought about suicide. I need your help."

If you don't feel you can talk with your parents about this, or if you want to talk with someone else, too, talk with another adult you trust—a clergyperson, another adult relative, the parent of a close friend, a favorite teacher, or a counselor at school. If you don't have anyone else to talk to, you can call 1-800-442-4673. You will talk with a counselor who is trained to advise children about serious problems. You can call this number day or night. The call is confidential and will not appear on your phone bill.

You are not alone in feeling really bad and not wanting to feel that way anymore. All of us, at one time or another, feel very sad or disheartened. Everyone has problems, and no one's life is perfect. All of us have things about ourselves and our lives that we would like to change. Sometimes sadness and discouragement can feel so overwhelming that you don't want to deal with it anymore. But wanting to die isn't the answer. Talking with someone and explaining how you feel can be a very important step in improving your situation.

There are many ups and downs in life. Although you may feel as though you are in a very low place right now, it is important to remember that there may be an uplifting time coming up soon. In time (and especially with help from caring, trusted adults), low feelings pass. You may find this hard to believe right now, but you will be happy in your life and you will find peace.

Brandy, please know we care about you. We can tell from your letter that you are a sensitive person who knows that there are ways to feel better, and just needs help finding them. It shows maturity and wisdom to realize that you are having trouble dealing with a situation alone and that you'd like help in dealing with it, and then to ask for that help. We hope you continue to make such wise, healthy, and positive choices, and that you will talk about this very soon with adults who know and care about you.

Please write back to us if you need to.

Dear Highlights,

No one understands how much I love my dad. I cry whenever he drops me off at home after seeing him on the weekend. My parents are divorced. I see my dad every other weekend. Whenever I think about him, I cry because I am not with him. What should I do? Every time I call him, after I hang up, I cry because I'm not with him.

—Amanda, 1987

Dear Amanda,

It is natural for you to feel sad sometimes. Try to just enjoy the times that you do have with your dad rather than always thinking about how sad you are when you have to say goodbye. Save special school papers or news of things that have happened that you want to share with your dad the next time you see him. Call him up when there is something special you want to tell him right away. Try not to make it hard for your dad by spending all your time telling him how much you miss him.

Dear Highlights,

My dad always tries to find time to shame me, and it makes me feel humiliated in front of the family. I get speechless, and then he assumes that if I'm trying to ask for something, I don't have any good reasons. He always lectures me, always slaps me, and he shows love to my siblings but me, he just looks at me like a bag of smelly trash. I hate him, and I cry every day because he calls me stuff I don't want to say, and I hate him. I seriously do. Is that a problem? What can I do?

—Anonymous, 2016

Dear Friend,

You told us that your dad always slaps you. If he hits you hard enough to leave bruises, then it's important to let a trusted adult you know right away. You could talk to your mother or another adult relative, a teacher, coach, school counselor, or clergyperson if you attend a place of worship. These people care about you and may be able to give you some helpful suggestions. If you don't have anyone else to talk to, you can call 1-800-442-4673. You will talk with a counselor who is trained to advise children with family problems. You can call this number day or night.

If you feel safe doing so, you might want to talk to your dad about what's been happening. Timing is important, though. Try to find a time when things are quiet and your dad is not too tired or too busy to talk. You could say something like, "Could we talk about how we could get along better?" Listen carefully to what he says and try to stay calm. Instead of arguing, try to concentrate on hearing what he has to say. Then tell him how you feel, too. If the two of you can talk it over calmly, you might be able to work things out and get to understand each other better.

When you feel upset by what's going on, you can try to find a way to change your mood. You might write in a journal, work on a project, write a poem, talk to a friend, go for a walk or get some other exercise, or listen to some relaxing music. It can also help to have a strong focus on your schoolwork. Doing well at school can boost your confidence and help you realize that you are a good, capable person. Nobody else has the power to control how you feel, who you are, and what you think about yourself; those are things that you can decide on your own.

Remember, this isn't something you need to resolve on your own. We encourage you to reach out to the caring adults in your life and share your concerns with them. They can guide and support you as you work your way through this.

My MOM
Sweet, loving, caring.
   My MOM
loved, cared for, hopeful,
   My MOM
Sick, Dying, still Faithful,
   My MOM
A 32 Something,
A Dying thing going on
for ever unnoticed,
   My MOM
She is a box, A few
open her to see what's
inside, But Most judge her
by wood and paint,
   My MOM
A ghastly white
squiggly thing, tumbling
on forever, wondering
what She'll Never get to do,
   My MOM
She is eternal,
for after her human
death, She'll live on
For ever, happily, in Heaven,
She's My MOM and I Love
her.   (I wrote this y My MoM cuuse
         she has lympthoma, a type of cancer)

—Emily, 2007

305

Dear Highlights,

I am writing on behalf of my feelings, which are buried so deep inside of me, that I refuse to talk about it to anyone in person (except for one special person who recommended telling my problems to you.) My feelings are, well, down. Everyday, when I wake up to see the new sunshine pouring through the window of my room, I think, "What will today be like? Will I be made fun of today? Is life worth living after today?" My mom is hard on me and my life is like climbing a mountain when I'm pained greatly with hunger. My mom yells at me, tells me to do this and that, hits me sometimes, and does all these things for what reason, I don't know! I never want to talk to her about it because I know she won't listen, and she won't understand me. Sometimes, I feel that I am not loved anymore because my dad is hardly ever home, my sister will not listen to me, and all my relatives live overseas. I feel so terrible; I always think how unfortunate I am to be brought into this world twelve years ago. I have suffered torture almost all my life, and I have experienced it long enough to know life isn't worth living at all. I don't want to talk to my teachers about it, because I don't feel it is right to bring the matters of my life into the burden of my teacher's. Please help me in some way, which I can express my feelings without using words so my mom could understand how I feel. Thank you.

—Lara, age 12, 2000

Dear Highlights,
I know a classmate that is having some problems with her life so I suggested she write to you guys. Here is her letter.
PS: Please send your answers to my address.

—Nick, age 12, 2000

Dear Nick,

Thank you for convincing Lara to write down her feelings and for sending her letter to us. You must be a very good friend to her, and she is lucky to have you in her life.

We hope you will encourage her to talk to an adult and get the help she needs to feel better. Her problem probably won't "just go away." If she won't talk to an adult herself, you might want to discuss her problem with an adult you trust. Although doing that may seem like going behind her back, by getting her the help she needs, you are really being a good friend.

Dear Lara,

We're glad Nick convinced you to write to us with your problem. We are sorry to hear that you are feeling so sad and depressed. When you feel this way, it is easy to convince yourself that life will never get any better. But the truth is that there are many people in your life who care about you and want to help you feel better.

We suggest that you talk to an adult you know and trust. If you don't feel comfortable talking to your parents or your teachers, you might try talking to your school counselor or a relative. It is important that you let someone know how you've been feeling. If you don't have anyone else to talk to, you can call 1-800-442-4673. You will talk with a counselor who is trained to advise children with family problems. You can call this number day or night. The call is confidential and will not appear on your phone bill.

It may surprise you to know that most people feel sad or depressed at one time or another. The best way to help yourself feel better is to let an adult know about your problem. Keeping your feelings bottled up inside usually only makes you feel worse. Sharing your life and feelings with people who care about you (like Nick) gives them the chance to help you feel better.

Slim Secret

Please respond to this letter, my birthday's on October 22nd, and before I turn twelve I'm trying to lose ten pounds without my mother knowing.

She tells me I'm small considering I'm the size of a fourteen year old, it's been two days, and I've lost five pounds already, but I don't want her to find out.

She tells me I'm not big but I think I am, in the past two days I have eaten NO junkfood whatsoever, plus I've used a trampoline, I've taken video Michael Jackson dance classes, and I've lifted weights, it's very frustrating to keep shut around my mom, please help.

—Jessi, age 11, 2001

Dear Jessi,

We can understand why so many people want to lose weight. The pressure in our society to be thin is powerful. Many people are doing unhealthy things to their bodies just to fit the idea of what is acceptable as shown in magazines and on television. We hope you will remember that the people who promote the idea that only very thin women and girls can be pretty are not people who care about you. They are trying to make money.

Your mother loves you and wants what's best for you. We recommend that you talk to her about what you are doing right away. We're sure she will want to know about anything that's bothering you. She will certainly want to know that you have been working so hard to lose weight.

We are worried about you. We get many letters from readers who want to lose weight. Every doctor we have ever talked to about weight loss says that it is not healthy to lose weight as fast as you have been doing. We think it's great that you are exercising and being careful to eat only foods that are good for you, but you must be careful not to overdo it. Your mother and your doctor can help you figure out how to lose a healthy amount of weight, if any.

Dear Highlights,

My Dad is in jail and I'm really scared. I miss him so much. I want to see him but I can't. I'm really scared, and I'm really sad. I really need help. Could you please help me? I don't know what to do. When I look at pictures of my father and I cry. I just can't help it. My grandmother told me to cry until I can't cry anymore, It helps a lot. But I really do need your help. Please, please, please help me.

—Aaliyah, age 11, 2005

Dear Aaliyah,

We understand how sad and frightened you must feel right now. We are glad that you wrote to us for help.

We are sorry that your dad is in jail. We're sure that he loves you and misses you. People go to jail because they have made serious mistakes in their life. But a mistake can be a chance to make a change for the better. It may be that your dad will learn from this experience and will be able to have a fresh start when he leaves jail.

You might want to ask if you can write letters to your dad while he is in jail. Even though it is not the same as seeing him, keeping in touch through the mail can help you keep from missing him so much.

We hope that you will talk to your mom, your grandmother, or another adult you trust about how you feel. Talking to someone who cares about you can help you handle the painful feelings you have and help you not feel so alone. Keeping your feelings bottled up can make them even harder to deal with. Crying is one good way to let your feelings out, as your grandmother says. Talking to others so that you don't feel alone is another. If you don't have anyone else to talk to, you can call the National Youth Crisis hotline at 1-800-442-4673. You will talk with a counselor who is trained to advise children with family problems. You can call this number day or night. The call is confidential and will not appear on your phone bill.

Dear Highlights,
Lately I've been scared of thing that never scared me
before. Like death. I don't know how that kind of thing
came to mind. I would have little fright attacks and start to
shiver uncontrollably. My heat beat would rise and I would
get scared that my heart would just stop. Sometimes I get
pain in my chest like it was my heart hurting. My mom
says that its just my cold that I was getting over or either
growing pains. She also say that I'm very out of shape. I
know that I am out of shape because I don't play as much
as a kid who goes to regular school would. I do play but
just not very much. I don't like to worry about this kind of
stuff. My mom say that I will be a leader someday. But I
wouldn't understand how she can see that because leader's
aren't afraid. My mom always says "Just because your
afraid doesn't mean your not courageous. Courage means
to feel fear but do what you need to do anyway." Even
though she says that, I don't know how to overcome this
fear. Can you help me?

Pink + Purple = Pure Awesomeness!!! Also Known as Me!!
                                                    ~Ashti, 2010

Dear Ashti,

We're sorry to hear you've been feeling frightened and worried. It may help to know you're not alone. We're certain that everyone feels afraid sometimes—even people who are in leadership roles. Fear is a natural response to stressful thoughts or situations. We think your mom's advice about courage and fear is very wise. Just as it's possible to feel angry without lashing out, you can feel afraid while showing courage in your actions. It is brave to ask for help when you're upset or scared, so we're proud of your courage in seeking our suggestions!

One good way of dealing with fear is by sharing your worries with people who care about you. We hope you'll continue letting your mom know when you're afraid and asking for her support. You can also talk with your grandma, sister, or other family members. They may not always be able to change the things that are frightening you, but they can reassure you that, no matter what happens, they will love and protect you.

Your family doctor can be a good source of ideas, too. Your emotions are an important part of your health, and your doctor would want to know about any emotions that are causing you to feel unwell. The next time you have a checkup, maybe you can share this letter with your doctor. He or she may be able to recommend breathing exercises or other techniques for calming yourself during a "fright attack."

When you begin to feel nervous or frightened, you might try distracting yourself with a favorite activity. For instance, you could call a friend, play a game, read a story, or create a piece of artwork. Many people find that exercise is helpful in relieving stress. You don't have to be in perfect shape to exercise your muscles. Simply taking a walk or doing a few, simple stretches may relax your mood.

Dear highlights,
My dad has very bad habits. He likes to go to casinos, smoke, and drink. My family and I have tried talking to him about it. It never works. He doesn't say anything, he just keeps on doing bad things. I feel like I don't even have a dad. My mom is going back to college and she has to study a lot. Every time she tries to study, my dad gets drunk and yells for her to come in there. Sometimes when we leave he breaks things. Can you help us?
Your friend
and reader,

P.S. I can't even breathe because of the cigarette smoke!

—J. P., age 11, 2002

Dear J. P.,

We can tell that you are feeling sad about your dad's behavior and frustrated that talking to him about it hasn't helped.

It's important to understand that you can't change or control the behavior of others. They must want to do that for themselves. You can still show that you love and care about the other person, but you need to take care of your own life and to try to be happy. Developing a positive attitude isn't easy but it can give you the strength to make the most of your life.

One thing to help is to talk to people who care about you when you are feeling upset. We hope you will talk to your mother or another adult you can trust about your concern. This could be a relative, a teacher, a school counselor, or a clergyperson if you attend a place of worship. If you don't have anyone else to talk to, you can call 1-800-422-4453. You will talk to a counselor who is trained to advise children with family problems. You can call this number day or night. The call is confidential and will not appear on your phone bill.

You can also find out about an organization called Al-Anon/Alateen, which offers support to people whose lives are affected by the drinking of a friend or relative. Your mother or another adult, such as a school counselor, can help you find out more information about this organization.

Good luck. We care about you.

Dear Highlights,
I been getting bullied at school and I been getting called stupied idiot, big fat loser. I been telling the teacher but they aren't doing anything to make it stop and I been getting hit by other kids. Please can you make it stop!

—Serenity, 2017

Dear Serenity,

It's good that you've told your teachers what's happening. We encourage you to continue doing that.

We also encourage you to let your parents know who is bullying you and in what ways. If you are not getting help from your teachers or other supervising adults, then your parents may want to speak with your principal. It is their responsibility to make sure you and every student feel safe.

Dear Highlights,   4-2-99
         I was wondering if you could
write me back personal? Well, I have
a friend and she is very friendly and
nice but theres a problem. The problem
is that she has been doing things to me
and she says I love you but I do know
that it is not wrong to say. Well, one
day she put one of her arms on my
shoulder and she wanted me or should
I say inaway she wanted me to put
my arms around her waist. It short
of bugged me because I donot know
what she is trying to do. Sometimes
we hug in school + some of my
friends think I am going out with
her and it proably means goodbye
to her? She is a good friend.
Sometimes she says to her younger
sister (8) and to her best friend (10)
that we are going out with each
other About 15 times she has put her
arms around my waist because she
wants me to product her + to keep someone
way from her. 2 times she faked kissed
me + in front of her sister once. She
is 2 years younger than me. I
known her for 6 years. Ome of her
friends wrote her a note + I saw
what was on it + it had questions
for her to answer + heres some.
                                    →

Do you think ____ is cute for a guy? Her respond - yes if she was a guy. Do you think ____ is a Jibo? Her respond - yes.

If ____ wanted to kiss you will you let her? Her Respond - depends !!! °°°

What is ____ a guy or a girl to you? Her respond - a sister / boy / girl.

Will you EVER go out with ____? & Why & it can't be because she is a girl. Her respond - Maybe because ......

I think my friend is trying to make me fall in love with her. Maybe she is in love or she likes me.? It has been going on since November 16 '99

Please remember to write back personal.

—Crystal, age 14, 1999

Dear Crystal,

As long as you wonder why your friend is acting as she does, you're going to feel uncomfortable around her. We suggest that you have a talk with your friend. Find a quiet time when you can talk privately. If you have trouble bringing up the subject, you can say something like, "This is hard for me to talk about, but . . ." Once the subject is in the open, it will be easier to speak honestly about it. Explain in a calm, kind way why her actions make you uncomfortable. Listen carefully to what she has to say, too.

Remember that no one has the right to touch you in a way that makes you uncomfortable. Your friend may not know that it bothers you. Although it may seem difficult, we believe it's better to be honest about how you feel than to let a misunderstanding grow.

It might help to talk to your mom or dad about this. They would want to know if you are having a problem, and they may be able to give you some good advice.

What We've Learned

WHEN CHILDREN WRITE TO US TO SHARE THEIR HOPES and dreams, worries and fears, and questions about the world, we are honored to be invited into the circle of people they trust. To have been asked by so many kids for validation and direction is humbling, especially when we pause to reflect on how much we have learned ourselves from the very kids we seek to help. We gain from every conversation we have with a child. And we are left with a deep desire to amplify the voices of children so everyone who cares about kids can hear what they have to say. After 75 years of conversing with children, we can safely conclude that most young children yearn for more moments when the grown-ups they love are fully present and actively listening.

We've heard from enough parents over the years to know that our correspondence with kids has helped create more of those moments for their families. They tell us, and many of us know from our own experience, that raising children often feels like a juggling act. The need to find a lost shoe, run to catch the school bus, finish homework, or get dinner on the table can leave too little time for reflection and quality conversations with kids. But if our letters prompt parents to "clear the deck" for just a little while to have an important conversation with their children, it's a win. That's one reason why we take great care in responding to each child.

Although each response to a letter we craft is intended for the child, we can't know if other eyes will see it. With certain letters, it's especially important to consider this possibility and think about the consequences for the child. We never want our reply to make a difficult situation worse if the letter is seen by others for whom it was not intended. In most cases, however, we hope that parents and caregivers see what we wrote to their children; because reading our exchange of messages might help them better understand their child's thoughts and feelings, adding clarity to a conversation a parent already had or will have with their child.

Even when caregivers are aware of what's on a child's mind, they may not understand the full weight of it. Occasionally, we hear from parents who tell us that our reply to their child's letter or email helped them understand the depth of their child's grief or the extent of their child's struggle. In 2020, eight-year-old Nick's mom thanked us for the letter we wrote to her son after he sent us a poem about the death of his grandmother. "His grandmother died this spring, and he's having a really hard time with the loss," she wrote. "Apparently he wrote a poem about her, and we didn't know. The kind letter you sent contained tips for helping him with his grief and letting him know that he will feel better over time. Thank you for taking the time to help a little boy going through a rough time losing his grandma." In 2016, a mother wrote to thank us for a thorough response to her daughter's letter. "You have given us much to think about," she wrote. "Kayla seems to treat other kids in a harsh or disrespectful way when she feels left out or overwhelmed by complicated social/emotional situations . . . I'm glad she at least feels bad about her behavior and wants to change. She decided to write to you all by herself . . . We will all keep working to get better." A father wrote to us after learning that his daughter had sent us a message about the family cat, which was dying. "My wife and I were unaware that Megan had written to you . . . Your letter was obviously personally written to address all the comments and concerns Megan had raised and gave wonderful advice about how she could help our pet be more comfortable and how she should talk to us. She was deserving of the attention you gave her. Thank you for recognizing that."

We've also learned that kids, although they may not have said so, tended to be appreciative of the listening ear and guidance they were offered. Some children write to us again as teenagers or young adults after remembering or rediscovering our original letter, which they had saved. In 2015, for example, we received a thank-you email from a reader who had written to us three years prior, afraid to tell his family that he was secretly learning the Russian language. He believed they harbored fear and prejudice against Russians and would be angry. In his second note, he let us know that he took our suggestion and talked to his family about his hobby, and that they were not offended. Relieved of the burden of secrecy and unnecessary guilt, this gifted young man continued to study Russian and also went on to learn Ukrainian.

Our mail also shows that no matter how loving and attentive their family is, a child can still find it difficult to confide in a loved one. Sometimes kids withhold because they don't wish to hurt their parents' feelings, or because they don't see a solution but simply need to feel heard. In 2012, Leslie's mom emailed us after learning that her seven-year-old had shared with us her wish for more of her parents' time and attention. Leslie understood that her little brother's autism was the reason for this family dynamic, and her letter to us helped her mother understand why Leslie was reluctant to share openly with her. "We are very busy taking care of and chasing after our son," her parents wrote. "That being said, WE LOVE OUR DAUGHTER TREMENDOUSLY. There are times we have to tell her that we have to attend to Kyle, and I think this may make her feel lonely. We have assured her we love her and don't want her feeling lonely." In another letter, eight-year-old Leah wrote to us without her mother's knowledge. "We've been struggling for years with intense behavioral issues that have, in turn,

Our mail also shows that no matter how loving and attentive their family is, a child can still find it difficult to confide in a loved one.

resulted in hours of therapy (for all of us)," her mother wrote. "When I found and read the email she'd written to you, it broke my heart to know that—despite our best efforts to protect her—she too is fearful of the things that make her different."

Our conversations with kids have deepened our appreciation for the value of writing notes and letters. We've learned that sometimes kids simply feel safer writing down their thoughts and feelings.

Our conversations with kids have deepened our appreciation for the value of writing notes and letters. We've learned that sometimes kids simply feel safer writing down their thoughts and feelings. Sometimes they need to do so for clarity or for practice talking about their difficulty. For some children, it takes more courage than they can muster to look a parent in the eye and share news they know will be distressing. This is how a former reader felt years ago when, as a ten-year-old, she wrote to tell us that she had been molested. In 2020, she wrote again to share her story and thanked us for help that we never actually delivered. "That night," she said, "I wrote you a letter, addressed it, and left it on the table for my mom to stamp and mail the next day. It was never sent.

Something told her to read it, and it was instead used in an investigation against the pedophile. Nothing ever really came of it other than 2 months in jail & being put on the registry, but it still helped—especially being able to get it all out and talk about it when I felt like I couldn't vocalize it. I hope you know how meaningful & lovely & helpful it is to give people hope through letters and in general. You probably do, but it really is wonderful. It makes me cry to think about how much it means to me. Thank you so much."

Whether a child's concern is big or small, unique or universal, serious or sure to easily work itself out, it's real to the child and matters deeply. Kids share, sometimes in an incredibly heartfelt way, because they need to feel safe, and their sense of safety comes from warm, responsive, trusting relationships. That's why we're always careful in every response to urge kids to talk, in person, to an adult they know and trust. When kids reach out to ask for guidance and adults show up to listen without judgment, addressing both the facts of the situation and the feelings attached, kids feel heard. They feel not only safe but also valued and understood. They are more likely to seek the help of adults again (and they will have good reason to), and they'll be more likely to treat peers and loved ones with the same respect offered to them.

Most importantly, we've come to see that in every letter about almost every subject over the years, there are implicit, overarching questions embedded within: *Do you care? Am I loved? Do I have a place in the world— a place in the lives of the people I love?* We hope kids believe us when we say in many more words: Yes. Yes. YES! It's the happy ending that writes itself when we give kids what they want most: more listening, more understanding, more connection, more love.

Acknowledgments

hildhood is a short, sweet season—the soil in which we plant the seeds for everything kids need to become independent, optimistic, and healthy adults. In order to grow and bloom, all children need, to varying degrees, the support of caring adults they can count on to listen, guide, and encourage them. I hope that this reminder is the primary takeaway for readers of this book.

Writers need this guidance, too. Certainly the need is not the same, but many times in this endeavor I found myself thinking of the African proverb "it takes a village." Just as children benefit from engaging with many caring adults, so did I benefit from the help of others who believed in the possibility that sharing what we've learned from our conversations with our readers could change the trajectory of some kids' lives.

The Powerful Legacy of Highlights for Children: This book, of course, would not exist were it not for the Highlights founders, Dr. Garry Cleveland Myers and Caroline Clark Myers—a husband-wife team of devoted educators who held a deep respect for children. After long careers spent teaching (and continually learning), they put everything they knew about kids, as well as their life savings, into launching a children's magazine that eventually became a cultural icon. Their dream child, *Highlights*, was and is a magazine that encapsulated their lifelong mission, which they described in each issue as helping kids "grow in basic skills and knowledge, in creativeness, in ability to think and reason, in sensitivity to others, in high ideals and worthy ways of living." The founders' core beliefs about what kids need to become thoughtful, literate citizens of the world are foundational to our work today.

The Highlights editorial office, located in Honesdale, Pennsylvania.

The Myerses did an exceptional job of passing on to their own children and grandchildren their sense of purpose. The company is still closely held by the family, which shares not only the pride of ownership but also the responsibility. Four generations strong, the owners take seriously their stewardship of an enterprise created to benefit children and families. Garry Myers III, grandson of the founders and CEO from 1981 to 2007, pushed the idea that family commitment to the enterprise was key to Highlights' survival, creating a Myers Family Council to keep the family close to one another and informed about the business. Today, the fourth generation leads the Council, and, following the example of their parents, they have documented in writing their intent to keep the brand family-owned, still believing that's the optimal way to position the company to serve future generations of children. Many members of both the third and fourth generations have served at various times as members of the corporation's board of directors.

The founders' core beliefs about what kids need to become thoughtful, literate citizens of the world are foundational to our work today.

Several family members have played even more active roles to ensure that the legacy of Garry and Caroline is ongoing. When their grandson Kent L. Brown joined the editorial team in 1971, he committed to the continuity of the editorial philosophy and was mentored by Dr. Walter Barbe, a well-known educator handpicked by the founders to succeed them in 1977. As part of his training, Kent answered countless letters from children. After becoming editor himself in 1980, recognizing how our reader mail uniquely revealed the inner lives of kids, he decided to begin saving all the children's mail we received. He formed a department to oversee the answering of letters and formalized the training of editors who wrote replies.

When Kent eventually passed the editorial baton to me, a few decades later, he invested time in teaching me more about the thinking of the founders and the core beliefs that guide the company. I'm grateful for his mentorship, particularly for all the hours spent on the porch of the founders' Pennsylvania home where the company frequently hosted Highlights partners and visitors. After dinner, we'd have coffee and dessert around the same table where the Myerses themselves entertained employees and distinguished guests—professors, clergy of various faiths, well-known illustrators such as Munro Leaf, and even their own beloved grandchildren, who visited every summer. A compelling storyteller with a great sense of humor, Kent would talk about his grandparents' lives and work in a way that was warm and personal —and also inspiring.

Although Kent, for many years, may have been the primary

> A compelling storyteller with a great sense of humor, Kent would talk about his grandparents' lives and work in a way that was warm and personal— and also inspiring.

storyteller of corporate history in our editorial offices, he is quick to say that the narratives of his cousin, Patricia Mikelson, should be considered the most factual. Pat is the eldest daughter of Mary and Garry Myers Jr., who played pivotal roles in the company's earliest days before perishing together in a 1960s plane crash. She always held a special interest in our corporate history. In the 2000s, Pat dived even more deeply into the Myerses' own writings and traveled around the country to collect the stories of people who played important roles in the company's early days. After she became the official family historian and company archivist, she extended the efforts of Kent to save the letters, poems, and drawings from kids by working closely with The Ohio State University to collect and preserve them. The hope was that researchers would find the collection easy to access and helpful in their study of American childhood. Pat's dedication to and passion for this project inspired many members of the Myers family, as well as of the

The hope was that researchers would find the collection easy to access and helpful in their study of American childhood.

corporation, to join her in financially supporting the initiative with ongoing donations. (For more on The Ohio State University archive, see page 334.)

Arguably, the practice of answering every letter and email from children does not favorably impact the company's bottom line over the short term. But the practice continues today with the enthusiasm and full support of CEO and Myers great-grandson Kent Johnson. Kent's own appreciation for

reader mail took root when he learned to answer kids' mail as an editorial intern on summer break from college. He went on to become a physicist with a doctorate from Harvard.

But in 2004, he left the world of science to work for the company again, soon moving into the role of CEO. Few people talk with his zeal about our vision for a more optimistic, empathetic world. Over the years, I've appreciated his support of me personally, his respect for the work of Editorial, and how he speaks from the heart in his frequent reminders to the entire organization that we do the work we do to help kids become curious, creative, caring, and confident.

To those who helped me bring this legacy to life on these pages: I often describe Highlights as a company where the goodness both trickles down and bubbles up. It's been a joy to work with individuals up, down, across, and throughout the organization who embrace our mission and are thrilled to be playing a role in helping kids become their best selves. I'm grateful for the guidance and support of two of the smartest publishing professionals I've ever known: Highlights executives Mary-Alice Moore and Liz Van Doren. Additionally, it has been a pure pleasure to work with the editor of this book, Marlo Scrimizzi. With deep thought and careful attention, she worked closely with me to choose the selection of letters, poems, and drawings included here. With patience and understanding, she was with me all along the way as I deliberated over word choices and turns of phrase, sharing my commitment to get it right.

Marlo's sensitivity and editorial instincts were also helpful as we reviewed the feedback from the many subject-matter experts who read an early-stage manuscript. Consistent with our longtime practice of consulting with experts when discussing sensitive or complex topics, we asked these professionals in various areas of childhood and child development to review my chapter introductions. I'm grateful for their willingness to share their perspectives, which always broaden and deepen our understanding of kids and help us be of even greater support to kids and parents. Thank you to Jennifer Miller, an educator/researcher with special expertise in kids' social-emotional development and founder of Confident Parents, Confident Kids; Dr. Chuck Herring and Dr. Christine Herring of Herring Seminars, Inc., experts in Diversity, Equity, and Inclusion; Dr. Natalia Ramos, Assistant Clinical Professor of Psychiatry at UCLA and a child psychiatrist with a specialty in LGBTQ+ services; Parker L. Huston, PhD, Pediatric Psychologist at Nationwide Children's Hospital and Clinical Director of *On Our Sleeves*; Dr. Alice Sterling Honig, Professor Emerita of Human Development and Family Science at Syracuse University; Dr. David Tranter, Associate Professor of Social Work at Lakehead University and Scientific Director at The Centre for Relationship-Based Education; and Terry Thompson, author, educator, and literacy editor at Stenhouse Publishers.

I am also indebted to two of the most reflective parents I know, who read early copies of this book and shared their perspectives: my friends Hillary Bates and Jessica Reesman Campbell.

Thanks to the Highlights colleagues who also read copy at various stages: Julie Beckman, our empathic, dedicated head of Human Resources; Sylvia Barsotti, an experienced editor in publishing for parents; and Andrew Gutelle, a highly creative writer and editor with an unparalleled ability to look at work in progress and accurately predict how readers will receive it.

Others who shepherded this book through its various stages are: Marie O'Neill, Highlights Senior Creative Director; design team Andrea Duarte and Carol Bobolts at Red Herring Design; Editors Christy Thomas, Katie Borne, and Laura Galen; Susan Jeffery and Laura Frazier Rice, who gave editorial support; Copy Editor Caitlin Conley and Managing Editor Rebecca Roan; Production Director Margaret Mosomillo, Production Manager Lauren Garofano, and Production Artist Jessica Berger. Each of these professionals worked their magic to ensure that the book beautifully reflects our vision and goals.

I'd be remiss if I failed to acknowledge members of the *Highlights* magazine staff over the years who have accepted the responsibility of answering children's mail and also the rotating roster of editors who handle the magazine column "Dear Highlights." Over time, we've learned well the art of choosing compelling letters about universal problems that will speak to a great many kids, editing them for publication, and then reducing our detailed personal replies to just a few sentences containing nuggets of good counsel. It's too difficult to name individually all the people involved in this important work, but Patty Courtright, who oversaw our Reader Mail department for more than 25 years, deserves special mention. With her knack for gently reminding busy editors of passing time, she made sure the flow of the outgoing mail matched the flow of the incoming. More importantly, she made sure that no letter was mailed before it was ready. Special thanks to editor Judy Burke, who has reviewed countless drafts of especially sensitive return letters over the last 20 years.

Finally, a very personal note. When I joined Highlights in 1994 and learned that answering children's mail would be an important part of my work, I felt my life was headed full circle. I was a kid who collected pen pals like trading cards, spent her babysitting money on beautiful stationery, and never balked at writing thank-you notes. This love of letter-writing has continued all my life, but I didn't expect that my appreciation for connecting through mail would only deepen at Highlights. I didn't expect that I would have the chance to view through the lens of an adult what I once saw through the eyes of a young person: the validation that rides along with a letter sent to a child from a caring grown-up. In my box of childhood keepsakes is a packet of letters from a favorite uncle, a quiet, introverted bachelor who attended to both a small farm and big thoughts. Always close, we struck up a conversation by mail that endured for several years, and, in his return letters to me, he encouraged me to think deeply about life's most important questions. I was fortunate to have a cadre of caring adults in my life, including my parents, but his influence was among the greatest. This was, in part, because I found it easy to reveal my inner thoughts via letters, but also because he took every question seriously and was honest and thoughtful in his replies. He didn't live long enough to meet my own children, but one of them shares his middle name. Whenever I wrote my kids letters—whether they were away at camp, on vacations with grandparents, and, later, far away in a college dorm—I thought of Uncle Dale. Today, when I answer children's mail on behalf of Highlights, I feel as though I'm paying forward the kindness and generosity of time and thought he extended to me.

My hope is that you, reader, may someday be privileged to receive a letter or email from a child who needs a listening ear. If you are so fortunate, I hope you will lean in and listen—and see the message as an invitation to be an important part of that child's life. Then I hope you will pick up your pen or seat yourself in front of your keyboard and write back with thought and care—and love.

My hope is that you, reader, may someday be privileged to receive a letter or email from a child who needs a listening ear.

With Deep Appreciation to The Ohio State University:

We remain deeply grateful to The Ohio State University for their thoughtful stewardship of our historical collection of correspondence. We are especially indebted to Dr. Eric Johnson, Associate Professor and Curator of Thompson Special Collections, and also to Rebecca Jewett, Thompson Special Collections Coordinator of Public Services. Their support and the help of library staff and students made it possible to efficiently access and sort through the vast collection of children's letters.

The flow of children's letters and drawings from Highlights to Ohio State is ongoing, but it began in 2008 with the eventual delivery of 12,000 boxes of children's mail, editorial correspondence with authors and illustrators, and all the documents related to the professional lives of the Highlights founders. This material might still reside in the attic and warehouses of Highlights had it not been for the enthusiasm of Dr. Joseph Branin, Director of University Libraries. After taking the time to listen to Pat Mikelson, Highlights archivist and great-granddaughter of the founders, when she made a cold call to him to gauge the university's interest in the collection, he agreed to the project right away.

The creation of the archive was the work of many hands. The gathering and packing of the boxes was a project of many months at Highlights, conducted primarily by Pat and her invaluable assistants Sharon Umnik and Laura Frazier Rice. The processing of the documents at Ohio State was started by Dr. Geoffrey Smith, Professor and Head of the Rare Books and Manuscripts Library, and Dr. José Diaz, Associate Professor and Curator of American History Collections. The work was later turned over to their associate Dr. Johnson, mentioned above. A number of other Ohio State staff worked to make access to the archive possible, including Cate Putirskis, Camila Tessler, Zoe MacLeod, Belle Teesdale, and Ashleigh Minor. Also instrumental were Ohio State University Libraries' Archival Description & Access Department student employees, who helped support collection access and cheerfully assisted the Highlights team researching letters in the library reading room. These students include Erica Alford, Kayla Bean, Emilio Bess, Emily Brokamp, Allyssa DiPietro, Sarah Fox, Connor Leckie-Ewing, Chloe Merriman, Clayton Mong, and Ruby Napora.

For information and permission to access these archives for research purposes, please contact Ohio State's Rare Books & Manuscripts Library at thospcol@osu.edu or 614-292-5938.

CHRISTINE FRENCH CULLY

An outspoken and trusted voice on issues that impact children and their well-being, **Christine French Cully** is dedicated to helping raise curious, creative, caring, and confident children, and to championing Highlights' belief that children are the most important people on earth. A writer, advocate for children, and longtime editor in chief of *Highlights* magazine, she is a frequent speaker at writers' and educators' conferences and the host of the *Dear Highlights* podcast.

Cully is sought-after for guidance on how to talk to kids about challenging topics, providing thoughtful advice not only to parents and families but to kids directly. She has personally answered thousands of their letters received at Highlights over the years and continues to do so every week. She compiled dozens of these letters in *Dear Highlights*, bestowing indispensable insight on kids' hopes, dreams, fears, and aspirations to the grown-ups in their lives.

Cully is the mother of two grown children. She lives in Nashville, Tennessee.